Airways and Airwaves ~ Stories I Tell to Friends

By

Captain David Gwinn

ISBN: 0-9772066-151500

Printed in the U.S.A.

W9-BON-322

Got a good story for Dave? It may make the second edition and be attributed. Send it to: dave@davegwinn.com.

Until then, until then…use your imagination and have fun!

FOREWORD
by Rod Machado

I still remember the time many years ago when I plunged into my mailbox, hand first, and pulled out a letter from Dave Gwinn. From that day on, I knew we'd be buddies for life.

I had just completed a video segment for ABC's *Wide World of Flying* on the type of clothing aviators should wear to minimize bodily damage in the event of a post-crash fire. With a blowtorch, and clothing laid out like a tiny flat pilot, I graphically demonstrated how assorted fabrics burned or melted at different rates. Upon opening Dave's letter my senses were assaulted by the strong scent of smoke. Since I do my own home appliance repair, I'm used to seeing lots of fresh-made smoke (and feeling electrical discharges, too). Nevertheless, the smell caught my schnozz snoozing. I removed his letter, which had burn marks and singed edges on all sides. As I recall, it began as follows:

> "I'm a little miffed at your recent video. I tried your techniques for not burning my shirt and trousers and hurt myself in the process. I'm in the hospital now. Thank you very much…"

Now that's a sense of humor that had me wearing a Gwinn from ear to ear. Thus began a wonderful friendship that has simultaneously satisfied both the intellect and the funny bone.

As you read this book of humorous aviation stories, you'll discover that Dave is not your average pilot. He's a flyer with a flare for fun. But this doesn't mean he flies funny. It means he sees things in a funny way, which makes him one of the most playful and humorous people I've ever known. That's why I never worry about his frequent attempts to steal my wife—my blonde bombshell. Yep, he's always sending her cute little notes like, "Why are you still with him?" and "You know he only loves you because you write all his books for him." Hmmm, now that I think about it, Dave's got his own blonde bombshell— Molly Jo—and she's a cutie, too. I just don't understand why he needs two of them.

Then there was the time I attended one of Dave's famous radar seminars in my hometown. I drove my new BMW to the event. That was a mistake. Dave later wrote my wife and said, "I saw Bubba's BMW for the first time. I got so tired of asking, 'Any questions?' and having Bubba raise his hand to ask, 'How many people know I have 16 speakers in my BMW?' Did you know that he drove it into the seminar room so everybody could see it?"

Those are the shenanigans that I, and all of Dave's friends, have had to put up with over the years…and we wouldn't have it any other way. At least now I think you have an idea of what's in store as you read *Airways and Airwaves ~ Stories I Tell to Friends*.

As you read, keep in mind that the ability to laugh is a disposition, while the ability to make others laugh is a gift. I am grateful to have such a wonderful, intelligent, loyal, kind and caring friend willing to share his incredible gift with me. Now he's sharing it with you, too. So read and enjoy this wonderful book, and don't be surprised if you learn one of life's most important lessons in the process. The hidden secret revealed in reading *Airways and Airwaves ~ Stories I Tell to Friends* is that it's possible to grow into adulthood, even to command a Boeing jet airliner, while retaining your childlike sense of play. By default, Dave's stories teach us to laugh, play and love life.

Perhaps Nicolas de Chamfort, the French writer, put it best when he said, "Of all days, the day on which one has not laughed is the one most surely wasted." Don't waste any more days. Read this book.

Rod Machado
San Clemente, California

FOREWORD
by Barry Schiff

I first met Dave Gwinn when he was teaching transitioning Boeing 767 pilots to understand and use flight management computers. This was in 1984. But Dave was like no other TWA instructor I had ever had. He actually kept us awake in his after-lunch class. It wasn't so much the scintillation of the subject as much as it was his finely tuned sense of humor. Dave kept us in stitches while skillfully and effectively teaching us what we needed to know about this revolutionary concept in navigation.

Dave had a knack for sensing when his students' eyelids were getting heavy and could arouse us from our reverie with clever and insightful humor that seldom veered from the subject at hand. (Most other TWA instructors simply ignored the sound of foreheads hitting wooden desks and continued unperturbed to instruct even though no one was sufficiently conscious to reap the dubious benefit.)

I recall thinking about Dave that he has the wit and wisdom to be a successful stand-up comedian. He is that good. He has a keen sense of what is genuinely funny and what is not.

As our personal relationship developed into close friendship over the years, Dave used his humor to help me through difficult times. He always had the time to cheer up a good friend even when his own troubles might have been more demanding.

It came as no surprise to learn that Dave had written a book of entertaining aviation stories, humor and anecdotes that he had amassed during his fruitful and lengthy career. I can think of no one more capable of such a task. And so it is that I leave you in the hilarious hands of my pal, Captain Dave Gwinn. Enjoy.

Captain Barry Schiff
TWA (Retired)
Los Angeles, California

Barry's Retirement. I followed six months later.

A viation has more that its fair share of characters, perhaps due to the high level of confidence and self-assuredness required to fill the very large shoes worn by airline crews of the preceding five decades. Amazingly, they endured impossible schedules flying temperamental equipment through all sorts of weather to amass a stunning amount of practical aviation knowledge, seasoned with random hilarity and occasional moments of sheer terror.

Captain Dave Gwinn is certainly no exception to this adventurous lifestyle, and can always be counted on to regale his listeners with riveting tales (mostly true) of his aviation experiences. Thankfully, he leaves this fascinating legacy in print for your enjoyment.

I am honored to have the privilege of working delicately with Dave's words, and even more so to be able to call him my friend. A finer human being you are not likely to meet.

Those who are meeting Dave Gwinn for the first time are advised to fasten belts low and tight, bring seatbacks to a full upright position, and hang on tight for a wonderful flight into Captain Gwinn's piece of the sky.

Cory Emberson
Lightspeed Editing
Hayward, California

INTRODUCTION

> The ultimate responsibility of the pilot is to
> fulfill the dreams of the countless millions
> of earthbound ancestors who could only
> stare skyward and wish.

M y tenure of aviation employment was marvelous: 1965 to 1998. In that time I was rated and/or instructed in single- and multi-engine airplanes, helicopters, gyroplanes, seaplanes, gliders, as an Instrument Instructor, and as an Advanced and Instrument Ground Instructor.

Before TWA, I enjoyed managing a 420-student flight school with nineteen great instructors, forty-three airplanes, seven college programs, VA training and a mechanic's school. As a brand-new instructor, now General Manager, I was nurtured and often guided by two superior instructors: Captain Bob Karlson (General Motors Flight Department– Retired) and Captain Bill Howell (FAA Flight Facilities– Retired). Their advice was always wise and freely given. Later I spent eleven rewarding years in TWA's pilot training center as an instructor and retired in late 1998 as a Captain on DC-9s/MD-80s. I had no desire to fly international. I just didn't have an eight-hour posterior for straight-and-level flight. Traveling the world now to teach seminars, I know I made the right decision. In business class, with TV, a good book, a sleeping pill and a big dinner, it is still a boring and unendurable ride across the pond.

After TWA I've been privileged to work for Honeywell Systems Training, traveling the world and teaching airborne weather radar classes to airline, corporate and military aviators. John DeVault, our manager, and Fred Polak, my direct supervisor, have been more friends than superiors.

Through my representative at Aviation Speakers Bureau, the wonderful Diane Titterington (www.aviationspeakers.com) has booked me at banquets, conventions, Sun 'n Fun, Oshkosh and many events where I've delighted to entertain and interact with pilots. Writing for many magazines I've come to know the finest editors in journalism: Lyn Freeman, Paul Bertorelli, Tom Haines and Paul Berge.

It was not only a marvelous career, it was fun. When I was fourteen, my father, an intense railway labor executive, said with sadness, "David, I worry about your future. You'd find something funny on your way to a homeless shelter." That was hilarious: *"What* is a homeless shelter?" A bit of a generation gap. Dad never fathomed how many times that ability to laugh allowed me to endure bad, sad, heartache times. Never trust anyone who doesn't know what's humorous. If you don't know what's funny, how can your perspective of what's important be relied upon?

I'm often asked if the burdens, the responsibilities of being an airline captain preys on one's serenity. I've always replied that "when you are qualified to do a job and want to do it, there are conditions that you willingly accept. Those are not burdens." From FDR to JFK, Bill Clinton and both Bushes: All thrived on the presidency, loved the action, the responsibility, the power and the life. LBJ asked us endlessly to pity his "awesome burdens in this lonely office." It's just a matter of seeking the job, willingly accepting the conditions that come with it and thriving on the challenge. When you're qualified to do a job, it's not a burden. Frankly, the cockpit was always going to get there with safety. If the passengers just kept their part of the airplane attached to mine, they'd join me in that safe arrival.

This small book originated with notes I kept over the years of the memorable, funny things that happened within a major international airline. The people I worked with (pilots, flight attendants, management, instructors) were creative, spontaneous personalities. There was always a day with laughter, even in the days of siege by Carl Icahn. Also included are notes, quotes, quips and jokes that entertained me during that time.

It all began in 1965 and meeting a fine instructor, Eddie Holloway. After leaving aviation and then retiring from the training department of a major corporation, Eddie returned to flight instruction. He does so now in the Kansas City area. In the 1960s the airlines required 20/20 vision. The industry was denied a fine pilot in the absence of Eddie. He launched many careers for others and was always enthused about the future aviation successes of his students. Thanks always, Eddie!

My deep affection for superb people I worked with and/or accounted to:

Chief Pilots Buck Pratt and Hugh Schoelzel; aviation consultant-author-best pal Captain Barry Schiff (www.barryschiff.com); my dear friend Rod Machado, brilliant and multi-talented author-speaker-pilot-educator (www.rodmachado.com); and memorable Captains Steve Lanard, Frank VonGeyso, Benny Clay, Clarence Powell, Jim Goodnow, Jim Elkan, Carl Eikost, Jim Comer, Dave Godec, John Prudhomme, Bob Dunham, John Wittenborne and Dana Haselgrove.

My abundant gratitude goes to my precious friend and editor, Cory Emberson, who affectionately needled me to finish this project, then polished it and contributed her own masterful grasp of verbiage and humor.

Dedication: The late TWA Captain Jim Mandigo, one of my best friends for thirty years, and with whom I pleaded not to take up skydiving. My fears were validated. I've missed him every day. And for John F. Miller and Wayne Vohland for reasons they well know.

More happily: For Molly Jo, my wife, the end of the rainbow, my best friend and my constant companion. Man does not live by bread alone, every so often he craves a cookie. Think Molly: Think laughter.

David B. Gwinn
dave@davegwinn.com

Rodistotle & Davinci

Rod Machado and I have appeared together at a few conventions. And, yes, that's our playful pseudonym for one another. At one hotel the restaurant was elegant, posh. The waiter was just too serious. So, with a straight face, I ordered the "Fill-et Ming-non". No smile. Rod likes seafood, so he ordered "May-Hi, May-Hi". We got a grin. I asked if they had any "Vishie-swish" as an appetizer, but if so, I wanted it immediately. "The last time they let it sit until it was cold!" Aw, yes, finally laughter.

At International Aviation Week in the Cayman Islands, Rod and I visited the huge sea turtle farm. Those monster turtles, believing they would be fed, were one on top of another, a mass of turtles. My creative pal remarked: "Wow, what a market for little turtle transponders!" Rod's imagination has been one of the delights of my life.

THE INFAMOUS LENS OF CAPTAIN JOHN

From the 1960s to my retirement in 1998, I enjoyed the friendship of Captain John. He's a big, affectionate, funny man with a pixie grin and a head of curly hair that will make him forever youthful. The story is sited at JFK International Airport when we were both probationary Flight Engineers. A probationary pilot has no recourse, no union representation. He may be fired "for cause" during that first year's employment. It was the most tenuous of times.

John was a Boeing 727 F/E. He had worked many years at the Overhaul Base in Kansas City and was himself a skilled mechanic. When seated at the Flight Engineer's seat, directly to the right is the circuit breaker panel on the aft wall of the cockpit. One can reach virtually any critical circuit breaker in an emergency to interrupt electrical power to a system. On that same panel is the test plug-in for the flight data recorder. One can plug in, listen to the noise and determine that it's working. Since it is a regulatory/legally sensitive device, a plastic flap protects the plug-in receptacle; lift it to expose the plug.

John had his friends at the overhaul base make a small adhesive sign: "Forward Lavatory Viewing Lens." On each flight he pasted it over the flight data recorder receptacle.

With the cooperation of the other two pilots, John awaited the arrival of a flight attendant sometime after takeoff.

When a flight attendant arrived, usually asking if they'd like coffee, the Captain would say, "John, I need to step back to the lav. Anyone in there?"

John would rotate in his seat, lift the flap, stare into an electrical socket and announce, "No, sir. It's empty. You can go on back."

You can imagine any flight attendant was aghast! "WHAT!? You can *see* into the LAVATORY?!?!?"

John would hasten to explain, "The *only* time we use that is for the Captain. He can't be standing in line back there. Besides, I never see anything."

In time they had all Boeing 727 flight attendants driven to using the aft lavs only.

One day, en route to a California layover, they have a bona fide hardened female as a flight attendant. They don't know that yet. The crew had dinner together that night. She wore white toreador pants and beneath them, polka-dot panties were evident.

The next day she came to the cockpit.

"John, I need to use the lav. Anyone in there?"

"No, sir. It's empty."

"What! I can't believe this! You can see into the forward lav?!"

"Well, we only use that for the Captain. He can't stand in line back there. Aw, shucks, we never *see* anything. I can't remember when I ever…well, yesterday I did see someone in there with polka-dot panties, but other than that, no one!"

She nearly broke the door leaving the cockpit. They got a good laugh out of it.

One week later, John found a note in his mailbox: "See me. Capt. Bill (Chief Pilot)."

This was an awesome threat for a probationary flight engineer. The essence of a successful airline career is to fly thirty years and never meet the Chief Pilot.

John reported to the Chief Pilot's secretary, who asked his name: "John." She stifled a laugh and pointed to the den of career-ending experiences, office of *THE MAN*. When John entered, Captain Bill was reading papers, head down and John waited patiently.

Captain Bill looked up and snapped, "Who are you?"

"I'm Flight Engineer John, sir."

"Are you the guy with *the sign?*"

John swallowed his heart. "What sign, sir?"

"The Forward Lavatory Viewing Lens!"

Choke! "Yes, sir."

"John, it's the funniest damned thing I've ever heard. I want to borrow it for a couple of weeks. I'll put it back in your mailbox."

John surrendered the sign and hastened to exit.

The secretary told him, "You need to hear the rest of the story. A flight attendant supervisor came storming up here with about ten young chicks in tow. She marched right into Captain Bill's office and demanded, "What is this modification on the Boeing 727?"

"What modification?" asked Captain Billy.

"The Forward Lavatory Viewing Lens, sir."

"Well, I'm puzzled, ladies. Why don't you tell me about it?"

It didn't take many sentences for Captain Billy to understand the hoax.

"Let me look into this," Captain Billy offered. He turned, selected a large revision volume from his bookcase, examined many pages, and said, "Here it is. Modification 1969-140-A. But it says right here, "Not to be used for lewd purposes."

"WELL, THEY ARE! *THEY ARE!*" wailed the supervisor.

"Ladies," Captain Billy announced. "I have only a copy of the revision. I did not approve it. You need to speak to the Boeing 727 Flight Manager in his office down the hall. I'm sure he can explain all this to you."

As they left, Billy picked up his phone, dialed, and announced, "You aren't gonna believe what's headed your way. Just listen to them and when you've figured it out, decide where you'll send them next."

Two weeks later, John got the sign returned through his crew mailbox.

John learned to fly at Central Missouri State University. They had a big flight training department. One day he and another student debated whether a chicken could fly.

John took a chicken up to about 5000 feet in a Cessna 150, slowed the plane, opened the window and the chicken was exited.

"I pulled off the power, dropped the flaps, spiraled and slipped that airplane and there was NO WAY to keep up with the descent rate of that chicken! That was not a bird; it was a rock!"

John continued the descent, entered the pattern and landed the airplane. He noted a small crowd gathered nearby. John walked over and found them encircling one big splat of feathers and blood.

The Chief Instructor nudged John and said, "Darnedest thing you ever saw, John. This chicken just came spinning in out of nowhere."

Fortunately the NTSB does not get involved in such incidents.

This, however, is a *real* in-flight bird event:

"No Hablo English, Señor"

Few flights are as saturated with sweet sorrow as a Captain's retirement flight. Flying copilot with a retiring Captain always motivates everyone to make it memorable, fun and to express appreciation to one's mentor. That was my good fortune with "Mike," a thirty-year airline veteran, former military fighter pilot with 118 missions over Viet Nam, Kentucky tobacco farmer and genuinely nice fellow.

We had one leg to Washington, D.C. with a twenty-hour layover, before continuing to Miami and back to St. Louis. It was always my practice to extract the names of the flight attendants from the computer for the whole trip and add them to the Welcome Aboard notice for passengers. They were part of the crew and should be recognized as such.

En route to DCA I commented, "Mike, look at this. All the flight attendants out of DCA have Hispanic last names." He shrugged. I thought it was interesting and unusual.

At the hotel Mike retired to his room, and I visited the courtesy crew room for the refreshments the hotel provided. As I entered, four uniformed TWA flight attendants were present and chattering in Spanish at a Mach

2 pace. I paused to listen to two lovely ladies and two male flight attendants.

Pretty Aquilla looked up, laughed and said, "Hi. We only get to practice our Spanish when we work with Paco and Pedro." The lads were obviously Hispanic and Cuban, as I learned. Paco was a small fellow, bland face, who reminded me of Stan Laurel in the Laurel and Hardy comedy team. The two ladies had Hispanic last names of some historic genetics and not of any recent ethnicity. All four were delightful people and we introduced ourselves. The idea light illuminated.

"This is Mike's retirement trip. Tomorrow morning *none of you speak English*. I'll handle him. Do not violate the script." They were tickled.

I had to alert Mike of this unusual situation. He was unimpressed. "Mike, they do not speak English. We may have a problem." He asserted that he'd appraise that tomorrow. The bait now had nineteen hours to ferment.

We were in the lobby the next morning, in uniform and awaiting the crew van, when Paco and Pedro arrived: *"Buenos Dias, el Capitán! Estamos sus prupo canban para este viaje."* Mike stumbled, mumbled some reply and simply studied the two. Pedro stated something in Spanish and moved to the coffee table. Mike wrinkled his brow and said not a word.

The two ladies arrive: *"Buenos dias, el Capitán."* Mike nodded hello. *"Puedo obetnerle algun café y un panecilo, Capitán?"*

Mike's eyes widened. "She wants to know if you want coffee, Mike," I suggested. He shook his head slowly.

As they left our presence, Mike grabbed my sleeve, pulled me behind a pillar in the lobby and exclaimed, "These people just got off the ^@*$%! boat!!"

I reminded him that his attention had been called to this problem the evening before. "What do you want to do, Mike?" He walked off muttering.

In the van, Mike sat in the passenger seat. All four sat behind him babbling Spanish at a torrid pace, pointing at Mike (beet red) and giggling. Small Paco said something to me. I replied, "Ah…no hablo Spanish." He replied, "Okay, me no hablo Inglish." Mike is about to convulse.

The Spanish continued from the moment they entered the van until they got their luggage at the airport and bid *el Capitán* a temporary good-bye: *"Uste veremos en el aeroplano!"*

Mike was livid! "Do you know what is going to happen if the FAA is on that plane? These people can't even read an announcement! This is my damned retirement trip. I'm supposed to be enjoying myself!!"

I said, "Come on, Mike. They had to read the announcements to graduate from the flight attendant training." He agreed they probably did.

"However, Mike, I'll bet they don't know what they're saying. It is probably all just phonetics to them." Mike's face sagged in defeat.

After he reviewed the release and weather, he handed the papers to me with the instructions: "I want four new flight attendants. I am *not* going non-routine in Washington on my retirement trip. Let's get to JFK. When you are in range, call them and tell them I want four new flight attendants waiting for us, no questions asked, no argument. Damnit, this is my *retirement trip*. I'm supposed to have fun!"

Those kids grabbed the whole idea and ran with it. The two ladies were well up into the jetway greeting all the passengers in English and assigning seats. Little Paco was standing in the cockpit doorway greeting everyone in Spanish. Mike was in the Captain's seat with his head in his hands. I stayed busy with my head down in my flight bag because I can no longer keep a straight face!

Paco entered the cockpit: "*Café, Señor David?*" Yes, please.

"*Leche?*" No, thank you.

"*Café, Señor Capitán?*" Mike mumbled yes.

"*Leche? El Capitán?*"

Mike snapped, "WHAT?"

Paco: "*Leche?* Er…ah…*leche.* El Capitán…"

Paco pretended to milk a cow and bellowed, "Mooo…Mooo."

Mike lost it: "No…no coffee. No nothing. Leave the cockpit. (pointing) I don't want anything!!"

All four flight attendants crowded into the cockpit, now rattling Spanish like the conquest of the Alamo. Mike is beside himself. "I can't understand a THING you people say!"

Aquilla handed him a card: *"Para El Capitán,"* kissed him on the cheek, and said, "We just said: 'YOU'VE BEEN HAD, Mikey.'"

Mike was doubled over in laughter. Those kids arranged cake, cookies and punch for us in Miami, Mike's last station stop. He admitted this was the finest memory he could summon up in this career. We took lots of pictures to assure he didn't forget.

Our arrival in St. Louis was at a time well into the Carl Icahn ownership of TWA and staffed with his management choices. Not one management member met that flight. Mike and I walked to the office, where we left all of his manuals and then walked together for his commuter trip home. I'm glad we made that retirement trip memorable. His career, flawless and admirable, meant nothing to Icahn and the caliber of people he selected as management. Thirty years. Not even a thank you or expression of good wishes for the future.

Asiana Airlines (emphasis is mine):

Safety

<u>If</u> you are sitting in an exit row and you can not read this card or can not see well enough to follow these instructions, please tell a crew member.

安全
安全
안지

非常口の隣にご着席で、英語がおわかりにならない方は、乗務員にお申し出ください

您若坐在走道位子面且不懂英文,請告知本機服務員。

조사 조애 뭐요 앉고 영어로 앉면지 못한
그러면 11 말씀하십시오.

Sicherheit Wenn sie neben einem ausgang sitzen und sie verstehen

THE INFAMOUS CAPTAIN DONNY,
ROGUE AND CLASS ACT

Captain Donny was a legend. His antics were classic, deserve airline immortality, and could fill a book. In fact, Don was incredibly smart, surely functioned with an awesome IQ, and he was usually just bored. Don thoroughly knew the regulations, flight operations policy manual, and all the guidelines. As he said once, "If you don't know the rules, you don't know how to break them with skill."

I first met Don as his flight engineer on Boeing 707s, based in San Francisco. Seated at my panel, a hat first came flying through the door past me: "Damn hats! I hate hats!" Don entered, vigorously tugging off his tie, hurling it too on the floor in the rear of the cockpit: "Damned ties! I hate ties!" He sat down, put on his oxygen mask, and yelled, "HELP!" as a pre-flight test. Don turned, looked me and tapped his empty shoulder straps: "You know why I don't wear the Captain's four stripes on my shoulders?" No, sir. "Because *I know* who is the Captain."

That was the beginning of a long friendship and many memories of laughter.

The Chief Pilot at San Francisco, Captain Jack, was watchful when it came to Captain Donny. Catching Don in one of his antics was a challenge. Don avoided Captain

Jack by wide margins. We were required to file a contact phone number with Crew Scheduling where we could be reached for emergency staffing, schedule changes or any other reason. They had badgered Donny for months, always getting his assurance that a number was forthcoming, but it just never did. Don was getting a divorce, or recently so, and was as transient as a homeless person at that time.

One day the Crew Schedule Supervisor remarked, "Don, we need a contact number by this afternoon or we'll refer it to Captain Jack and you can deal with him."

"Wow!" Don replied. "You'll have it this afternoon!" Within the hour he did just that.

It was many weeks before they needed to use that number. Back in those days Crew Schedule was not required to identify themselves to whomever answered. The receiving phone rang and rang...and rang and rang. When answered, it went like this:

"HELLO!"

"Yes, we're trying to reach Captain Don _____."

(Snarling) "I don't know if he's here. I'll check."

Long pause: "I can't find him. He's not here."

"This is TWA Crew Scheduling. Who is this, please?"

"THIS IS CAPTAIN JACK."

"Where the hell are you, Jack?"

"I'm twenty feet away from you at the pay phone in the hall. The damn thing wouldn't quit ringing."

This exchange meant one more reprimand for the Rogue.

There was one trip that I was scheduled to fly with Captain Don, on a beautiful California day, to the East Coast where weather appeared equally delightful. I arrived at Check-in in a tropical uniform, newly pressed, prepared for any inspection. Don was signing in, long blue uniform overcoat, buttoned to the collar. ("Well, I guess there is something that Don knows and I don't. Guess I should have worn a coat.")

Once in the cockpit, Don again hurled his hat across the deck: "Damn hats! I hate hats!" He whipped off the overcoat to reveal blue slacks, checkered sports coat, dress shirt and dark tie. "I've got a date waiting for me. I don't have time to change when we get there."

Don knew that contract: CBA, Collective Bargaining Agreement, negotiated by ALPA (Airline Pilots Association). It was the rules we worked by, the penalties and procedures detailed in specifics. One of them dealt with "Termination." To fire a pilot required notification under Rule 21A, an investigation announcement. Following that was a meeting with the company and union representation. This, in turn, was followed by an appeals process through many layers. In summary, termination was not viewed lightly, and went through many checks and balances. (The company always won anyway.)

Once in New York and flying Boeing 747s, the legend attributes another antic to Don, although he claims it was another Captain. Whomever it was (and Don is a likely candidate), he quickly alienated the Chief Pilot there as well. Captain Bill was short in stature and shorter in fuse. It is long forgotten for what purpose or what infraction, but Don was summoned to the Chief Pilot's office. In short order, however, feisty Don had baited Captain Bill to rage.

"I've had it! You're FIRED, Don. You're FIRED!!!"

Don could only shrug. "Well, okay." He hung his head and humbly left.

Don put a hold on his mail, unplugged his telephone and headed for Honolulu. The company spent well over a week calling his home, and even sent agents to knock on his door, sent registered letters, and still could not contact Captain Don.

Perhaps two weeks later, Don phoned the Chief Pilot. "Captain Bill, I've been thinking about this. I don't think you can fire me like that. Don't I get a hearing or something?"

Conclusion: back to work. Back pay for the *misunderstanding*. A well-rested Don.

Captain Don was summoned again, just before retirement for Sick Leave Abuse. Under the Icahn regime this was a major harassment of pilots. Statistically only 5% of pilots were abusing sick leave. Nonetheless, a policy of harassment assured that the other 95% would not subject themselves to the indignity of a lecture. Icahn's policy actually encouraged them to fly sick rather than endure the embarrassment, the childish rug-dance before the Chief Pilot to explain an absence. Three absences and you were on the carpet, whether it was three five-day trips or three one-day trips. A silly, destructive management technique when pilots had contractually up to two months absence fully covered under the contact for illness.

Don listened quietly while his absence was reviewed, while counseling was suggested for any health supervision that might *help* the pilot, and the company policy was outlined. "Of course, we do not want you to fly sick, Don. We are interested in your health." It was the usual phony sincerity masking the harassment. "Do you have any questions, Don?"

"Yes, I'd like to get paid two hours for this meeting."

"You *do not* get paid for a disciplinary meeting, Captain!"

"I came all the way from California for this meeting."

"You came today to fly your international trip tomorrow, Don. We had the meeting today because you would be in New York."

"So you're not going to pay me?'

"NO!"

"It's not fair!"

"You're not getting paid!"

"This is so unfair." Don got up. "This really makes me sick."

"That's the way it is, Captain. Let's have no more conflicts."

It took about two hours before the Assistant Chief Pilot realized what Don had remarked: "This really makes me sick." He called Crew Schedule. "If Captain Don calls in sick, I want to know." Answer: "He already has. About two hours ago." Don wasn't even out of the building before he used a pay phone to vacate the trip and return home.

There's more about Captain Don, one of my all-time favorite personalities and friends. I'll include it under another Favorites title.

This proposal always reminded me of Captain Don:

THE SLIP VALUE

K MCI 200153Z 01005KT 10SM 07/01 A3010 SLP196.

That was the new METAR or current meteorological report for airports introduced shortly before I retired. This happens to be Kansas City (for you non-pilots), at 0153 Zulu time on the 20th, with N-NE winds at 5 knots, 10 miles visibility, temperature 7 degrees Centigrade (1 degree dew point), altimeter 30.10 and lastly *Sea Level Pressure* 1019.6 millibars, underlined only for your attention. It was not fun to learn a new format after so many years, but we had to do it. That's not the story!

Notice the SLP at the end of the report. I advised a new young copilot that it represented "the SLIP value for the landing." It took an explanation: "You take your slip value of 196, subtract your landing weight in thousands, divide by two, then subtract the runway upon which you're landing. You'd like to have a value greater than 25. In example, 196 minus our 98 (98,000 pounds) divided by two and landing on Runway 30 all resolves to a slip value of 19. This will be a challenging landing."

The young lad sat quietly, looked at the report and said with both timidity and respect, "Sir, I really think that's Sea Level Pressure."

I snatched that report from the console, studied it for a minute (not a hint of a smile), and snapped, "ARE YOU SURE?!?"

With all courtesy he said, "Yes, sir."

I tossed it back with disdain and said, "Well, hell. Just forget it then."

It took him a couple of days to discover the playful personality in the left seat.

Retired Lieutenant Colonel Ron Ratliff, then a first officer, and I took it to a new level with a jump-seater in the cockpit. Ron reported a "slip value of 45, Captain."

I said, "Now, Ron, you've done it again. You subtract the weight, divide by two and subtract the runway value. You continue to subtract the weight and *add* the runway value."

Ron replied, "Well, Dave, I'm really sure I'm right. You *add* the runway. We've been over this before."

I snapped, "You may be right, but I'm the captain and we're going to do it my way. Now subtract the runway value and give me the figure. We'll discuss it later."

Ron computed all the figures, laid the square sheet on the console, and we obliquely watched our jump-seater. That relatively new captain was leaning forward, studying that sheet of paper, and trying to decide whether he had something to learn or he was riding with the two biggest idiots in an airline cockpit. He said not a word.

THE CO-PILOT (AS DEFINED BACK IN THE PROP DAYS)

I am the copilot. I sit on the right.
It's up to me to be quick and bright;
  I never talk back for I have regrets,
But I have to remember what the Captain forgets.

I make out the flight plan and study the weather,
Pull up the gear, stand by to feather;
Make out the mail forms and do the reporting,
And fly the old crate when the old man is snoring.

I take the readings, adjust the power,
Put on the heaters when we're in a shower.
Tell him where we are on the darkest night,
And do all the bookwork without any light.

I call for my Captain and buy him Cokes;
I always laugh at his real corny jokes,
And once in awhile when his landings are rusty,
I always come through with, "By Gosh, it's gusty."

All in all I'm a general stooge,
As I sit on the right of the man I call "Scrooge."
I guess you think that is past understanding,
But maybe some day he will give me a landing.

—Keith Murray

UNDERSTANDING RANK

The International Captain:

L eaps tall buildings with a single bound,
Is more powerful than a locomotive,
Is faster than a speeding bullet,
Walks on water,
Dictates policy to God

The MD-80/B-737 Captain:

Leaps short buildings in a single bound,
Is more powerful than a switch engine,
Is just as fast as a speeding bullet,
Walks on water if the sea is calm,
Talks with God when approved by crew schedule.

The Co-Pilot:

Leaps short buildings with a running start,
Is almost as powerful as a switch engine,
Is faster than a speeding BB,
Walks on water in a swimming pool,
Listens to God.

The New Hire Co-Pilot:
Runs into buildings,
Recognizes locomotives two out of three times,
Can fire a speeding bullet,
Keeps head above water,
Mumbles, mostly to animals.

The Senior Female Flight Attendant:
She lifts buildings to walk under them,
Kicks locomotives off the tracks,
Catches speeding bullets in her teeth,
Freezes water with a single glare.
She IS God!

———

Rod and I have shared many great aviation experiences together.

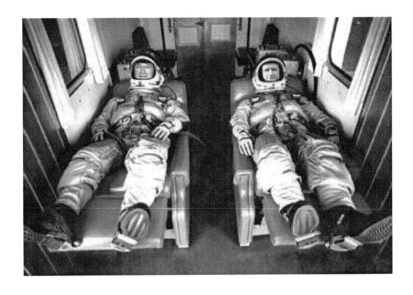

THE MAD HATTER

Captain Ed was a splendid pilot, splendid company and had only one glaring idiosyncrasy: He went orbital if he saw a pilot in uniform and without a hat. Ed could be in the midst of a cockpit joke at the ramp and interrupt himself to slam his hand on the glare shield: "LOOK at that! No hat!" Pointing to someone walking on the ramp: "That makes me so damned mad. No pride. No respect for his appearance. NO hat!!" Ed would turn as red as the TWA logo.

We flew the same trip for the month. With three hours of time to waste in Chicago, we normally went to the crew restaurant and then loafed in the crew lounge before continuing to Albuquerque.

It was time to leave and Ed could not find his hat! He collected every Captain's hat that he could find in the ramp office, called out names from the business card within them, distributed the hats, and finally had the hat with no Captain present. He was livid.

Ed charged up to the Flight Information Counter, slammed the hat down and bellowed, "You send this inconsiderate, irresponsible &^$#*!^ a long-line message and tell him to get my *&^%$*@# hat back here immediately. I ought to throw his damned hat away!"

Ed picked up his flight bag, nodded sternly to me to follow and headed for the gate. He had no hat, of course.

Walking down Concourse G, I lagged back from Ed. Gaining distance, soon I was at least fifteen feet behind him.

Ed turned and snapped, "Are you coming or not?!"

"Gee, I dunno, Ed. I hate to be seen with you not wearing a hat!"

There was a trickle of a grin. He turned, continued down the Concourse, and stopped at Gate 12 to visit with the gate agent. I hurried on board the airplane.

Obviously, I got to the cockpit and therein, the microphone and radio before Ed. He boarded, hung up his coat, placed his flight bag beside his seat, took his place, grabbed the microphone and said: "Clearance Delivery, TWA 414, IFR to Albuquerque."

Response: "I don't know, Captain Ed. We're not supposed to give you a clearance without a hat!"

Finally I'd gotten the good old boy laughing!

The next week, leaving Kansas City, I ran into Captain Al. "Give me one of your business cards, Al."

Back to Chicago and down to the crew restaurant. Ed tossed his hat up on the rack, I drifted back again. I took down Ed's hat, removed his business card, inserted Al's and joined Ed for breakfast.

When I arrived on the airplane, Ed was trying on that hat, removing and examining it, placing it back on, shaking his hat (to test the fit) and removing it again for inspection.

"What are you doing, Ed?"

"I've got Al's damned hat!"

"Isn't that the same act last week for which you called another captain an irresponsible, inconsiderate %$#@*&??"

Ed nearly shouted, "I haven't even *seen* Al today!"

"Well, hell, you must have, Ed. You stole his hat."

At altitude Ed often examined the hat. "It's got a break in the bill just like mine."

I replied, "They all break there, Ed. Lots of captains complain about it."

The hat wasn't much more conversation for the rest of the day. We did notice Ed inspecting it occasionally.

The next morning I arrived for the crew van, transportation to the airport from the hotel. Ed was seated in the front passenger's seat. His hat was on. He was staring forward. He did not acknowledge my arrival.

"Good morning, Ed. Did you ever figure out how you got Al's hat?"

Ed spun around, locked those icy blue eyes with mine, began the color transition that indicated his anger, and stated, "What I have, young man, is Al's *business card*. Thanks for asking."

I conclude that gentleman Ed, while on the layover, called Captain Al to apologize for taking his hat. As the years went by, Ed enjoyed the story as much as anyone.

Ed is retired now. His son was the youngest Captain on the airline for many years and never owned a hat.

Nothing was more discouraging than to finally upgrade to Captain and then have schedule reductions, planes parked or some malady by which one was returned to the first officer's seat. Eventually, of course, they made it back to the left seat.

Seen on an airline bulletin board:

"Will Trade: Captain's hat, size 7¾ for one First Officer's hat, Size 7."

We always found the propensity to wear a hat was inversely proportional to the amount of hair found on the pilot. Lots of styled hair…no hat. It seemed like the bald ones wore their hat all the time. Frankly, I wish all pilots realized how silly it looks to walk the terminal with a hat strapped to their flight kit, or as Captain Ed said and was correct, how unprofessional they appear. In an emergency and in the cabin a hat may be the only distinguishable feature of pilots directing survival actions. Any airline has the right to package *their own product*, and the professional appearance of pilots is part of that.

There were two airlines whose pilots had virtually identical uniforms. Obviously, it was difficult to distinguish between the two as a captain learned in stopping *another* airline's first officer in the terminal:

"Where is your hat?"

"In my flight bag."

"Why aren't you wearing it?"

"It's too small."

"So get a bigger one!"

"It wouldn't fit in my flight bag."

—Thanks to retired Captain Tom Travis, American Airlines

To another pilot whose hat was in his flight bag, the Chief Pilot directed:

"Either put your head in that flight kit or put your hat on your head!"

===—=

What financially devastated the airlines the most? It was the new, upstart carriers with little overhead:

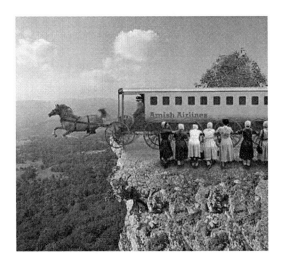

Aviation Clichés

A checkride ought to be like a skirt, short enough to be interesting, but still be long enough to cover everything.

<hr />

No one has ever collided with the sky.

<hr />

The propeller is just a big fan in front of the plane to keep the pilot cool. The proof? Make it stop, then watch him sweat.

<hr />

Rule One: No matter what else happens, fly the airplane.

Rule Two: Fly it until the last piece stops moving.

<hr />

Don't drop the aircraft in order to fly the microphone.

<hr />

An airplane flies by principles discovered by Bernoulli, not Marconi.

<hr />

The probability of survival is equal to the angle of arrival.

<hr />

The only time you have too much fuel is when you're on fire.

Three things kill pilots in Alaska: Weather, Weather and Weather.

Just remember when you crash because of weather, your funeral will be held on a sunny day.

Never fly in a cockpit with someone more brave than yourself.

Pilots and Air Traffic Controllers? If the pilot screws up, the pilot dies. If the controller screws up, the pilot dies.

Flying is not dangerous; crashing is dangerous.

There are more planes in the ocean than there are submarines in the sky.

Aviation has a perfect record—we've never left one up there.

Items of no value: The altitude above you, runway behind you, fuel still in the truck, approach plates in the car, the airspeed you don't have and 'half-a-second ago.'

If faced with a forced landing at night, turn on the landing light; if you don't like what you see, turn it off.

IFR checkride? One peek is worth a thousand cross-checks.

═ ═ ═

Never allow an airplane to take you where your brain didn't get five minutes earlier.

═ ═ ═

There are three simple rules to make a smooth landing; unfortunately no one knows what they are.

═ ═ ═

It's a good landing if you can get the doors open. It's a great landing if you can use the airplane afterwards.

═ ═ ═

After a gear-up landing, the last thing every pilot does before vacating an airplane is put the gear selection lever in the 'Down' position.

═ ═ ═

You know your landing gear is up and locked when it takes full power to taxi and it's quite noisy.

═ ═ ═

A smooth landing in a simulator is like kissing your sister.

═ ═ ═

See the propeller? Everything behind it revolves around money.

═ ═ ═

It only takes two things to fly: airspeed and money.

═ ═ ═

If God meant for man to fly, He'd have given him more money.

═ ═ ═

A fool and his money are soon flying more airplane than he can handle.

―――

When a forecaster talks about yesterday's weather, he's a historian; when he talks about tomorrow's, he's reading tea leaves.

―――

A terminal forecast is a horoscope with numbers.

―――

There are three ways to fly: the company way, the wrong way, and the captain's way. Only one way counts.

―――

Being an airline pilot would be great if you didn't have to go on all those trips.

―――

A copilot is a knothead until he spots opposite direction traffic at 12 o'clock; then he's an idiot for not seeing it sooner.

―――

A good simulator checkride is like successful surgery on a cadaver.

―――

The only thing worse than a captain who never flew as copilot is a copilot who once was a captain.

―――

Gravity: It's not just a good idea, it's the law.

―――

Helicopters do not fly; they are simply so ugly the earth immediately repels them.

―――

Basic Flying Rules:

1. Try to stay in the middle of the air.
2. Do not go near the edges of it.
3. The edges of the air are defined by the appearance of ground, buildings, sea, trees and interstellar space. It is much more difficult to fly there.

Without ammunition, the U.S. Air Force would be just another very expensive flying club.

The new FAA motto: We're not happy until you're not happy.

"My definition of an optimist has to be the Luftwaffe F-109 pilot who gave up smoking." (Capt. John Wiley)

Any attempt to stretch fuel is guaranteed to increase headwinds.

A thunderstorm is Nature's way of saying: Up yours!

Hovering is for pilots who love to fly, but have no place to go.

That just doesn't look right.

Big Mistake

The late Eddie Fisher was an aviation legend in Kansas City. He owned an FBO (Fixed Base Operation), three P-51 fighters, and his logbook dated flights far before my own day of birth. I liked that old grouch and spent many an evening in the QB fraternity with him.

The Story: Eddie had a minor heart attack and lost his medical. While he battled to get it back he, nonetheless, had to fly to various places for business. At the time I was managing a 400-plus student flight school next door to him. If Eddie needed to depart and be legal, he also needed a licensed pilot with a valid medical certificate in the cockpit. Eddie flew; his companion provided legality. He would often call me to see "if one of your students wants some Bonanza time" or "wants to go to St. Louis with me." They always did. It was easy to recruit a companion for Eddie. He did often let them fly the Bonanza.

One day I was in administrative havoc. Totally distracted, I accepted Eddie's phone call, promised him a pilot, and ventured into the pilot's lounge to find one. Hey, there's a chap I recognize readily. I asked if he wanted some Bonanza experience and invest some time in a trip to St. Louis and back. He was ecstatic. Problem solved.

About thirty minutes later I was looking out onto the ramp and noticed Eddie's Bonanza rotating on Runway 17.

"Hmmm, who was that kid I sent over there? I know he's our student and I readily recognized him. Oh WOW, I enrolled him last week as a student pilot! He doesn't have a license!" Eddie is betrayed and doesn't know it.

It was too late to call the tower with some excuse to summon the airplane back, so let's hope for the best. All the percentages were in our favor.

Later that day I looked toward my office door where the student awaited my attention. "That Mr. Fisher is sure strange."

"How so?" (Man, I'm glad you're back without an issue.)

"He asked me if I wanted to fly the Bonanza, which I surely did want to try. He had a single yoke and flipped it over to my side. I got us in a spiral. He was miffed, got it straightened out and gave me another chance. I did it again. He snapped at me 'How much flight time do you have, son?' and I told him eight hours. He didn't speak to me for the rest of the flight."

You can bet I didn't give Eddie a chance to speak to me either. I'm surprised he wasn't pounding on my door. When I saw Eddie, I made sure he didn't see me for a few weeks. He greeted me one day as if there was no issue and never had been. I don't know if it was charitable forgiveness or forgetfulness, but I was glad to have it behind us.

I never made that mistake again. Come to think of it, he never asked me for a pilot again.

THE FAA

I've had only good, the best of relations with the FAA in my flying life. Most of the inspectors I worked with in general aviation became friends, and many of my CFI contemporaries became FAA inspectors. I was only summoned to the FSDO office twice.

The first time was because of my own student, who declared an emergency ("Lost") on a CAVU (Ceiling and Visibility Unlimited) day over Lawrence, Kansas. The Kansas City skyline would have been visible and he was headed directly toward the airport. Nonetheless, he was scared and probably did the right thing.

I saw the school's airplane parked in front of the tower upon my arrival and wondered why. When I saw him seated in the inspector's office I had a clue. It was explained to me, and the lad's competence to be on the trip was challenged.

So I asked him, "What heading were you on?" 120°…direct to the airport.

"How much time remained in your computed flight plan?" Twenty minutes. Perfect.

I looked at the inspector and said, "Okay, he may never qualify for Mensa, but it's still possible to license him. Any issue?" None.

In 1969 Inspector Merrill gave me an ATP (Airline Transport Pilot or Almost Totally Proficient) checkride in a twin-engine airplane. Merrill was enjoying this. In a holding pattern he failed one engine and issued a climb clearance. Then he failed one VOR receiver. This was single-engine, single-VOR holding and a heavy workload (especially after he denied my request for priority handling).

Merrill failed the remaining VOR and issued an NDB clearance to MCI. On the way I turned on the cabin heaters and blowers on 'high.' This was on a 100-degree day in Kansas. In little time we are both sweat-soaked and the cabin temperature was intolerable.

Merrill: "Can you tell me any logical reason WHY we have the heat ON?!"

Me: "Yes, there are so many things failing on this airplane that I want every system operating. If they quit, I'll know."

That really tickled Merrill. I noticed he turned the cabin heaters OFF. Once we arrived at the LOM, he issued an NDB approach. We had an appreciable crosswind. As the needle flipped we hit one good jolt of radiation turbulence. Fantastic! The turbulence bounced my instrument training hood up and I could readily see the airport. It was an easy task to set up a splendid visual, crosswind final.

Merrill: "Okay, go around. That was pretty good."

Me: "Good, hell! That was perfect."

Merrill: "How do you know?"

Me: "'Cause I could see it as well as you could."

Merrill: "Let's go home. I give up."

At the KCK Municipal Airport, there was my all-time favorite FAA ATC controller, Bill. Gravel-voiced, tough as nails and a heart as big as the airport. He looked after the student pilots like a mother hen and recognized every instructor's voice. Bill and I often blazed trails in rustic terrain on dirt bikes, and somehow I was always the one getting hurt. (Bill died in May 2004.)

Coming from the west, it was procedure to report one's position relative to Wyandotte Lake (five miles out), then one mile west of twin-striped smoke stacks and from there to be filtered into the pattern. Bill and I had a litany that puzzled everyone.

"Howdy." (That meant I was over the Lake. "Howdy, y'all" meant I was one mile South.)

"One." (Report one mile west of the stacks.)

"I'll do it."

"I'm there."

"You're cleared." (I landed.)

On another occasion a student pilot gave Bill endless grief. Too fast in the pattern, then too slow. Final approach too far out, extending the pattern without reason. Finally Bill said, "Cessna 070, go around. When able turn to a heading of 270."

The student did so. After a five minute lapse of time or thereabout, we heard, "Fairfax Tower, Cessna 070."

"Cessna 070, Fairfax. Go away for a while. Maybe we can cooperate with one another later."

At the conclusion of Boeing 707 ground school, we had to take an oral exam on the airplane at the FAA Air Carrier Office. We were scheduled individually. There was one inspector who was known as a tyrant. Everyone feared being assigned to that guy. I got him. We were five minutes into a lengthy exam.

Him: "What's the power source for the fuel flow indicators and fuel flow impellers?"

Me: "The impellers are on P-5 and the indicator CBs are on P-4."

Him: "You got that reversed, but that's okay."

Me: "I don't think so." (Ohmagawd, did I say *that? He said it was okay.*)

Him: "Why don't we just look it up?"

He thumbed through a Boeing 707 manual, found his reference and shut the book.

Him: "You're right. When the examiner is wrong, the oral is over."

I had the acclaimed tyrant and the shortest oral exam of the entire class.

Few people were as quick with a retort as my pal Scotty. We had a bell (or more correctly a 'chime') system on the airplane. They had meaning. Typically you'd only hear three: Come to the cockpit. It usually meant the crew wanted a cup of coffee. (Four = Turbulence. Six = Emergency.)

One FAA inspector rode on Scotty's flight and said not a word. In leaving, I suspect he believed that he should have queried the crew about something.

"What's the meaning of six bells?"
Scotty: "Oh, I dunno. Two cups of coffee?"

At one time the FAA became rigid on inspecting revisions to manuals. We each had assigned manuals that were to be available in the cockpit. The Captain carried the Flight Operations Policy Manual. In the harshness of this supervision, the FAA was fining crewmembers $1000 for failing to update primary manuals.

The Inspector: "Captain, I see that Revision 106 is the last one in your FOP manual. Revisions 107 and 108 have been issued."

The First Officer: "Is that right? Let me look at mine. Damn, I'm missing those, too."

Guess who also got a fine for an un-updated manual that he wasn't even required to carry? If it was in the cockpit and might be consulted, it was to be current. Open mouth, insert Oxford, and we'll send you an invoice.

The last FAA Inspector to ride on one of my flights was a delightful chap. His origin was general aviation and we compared instructor stories. The flight attendant visited and asked if we had a beverage request. I took coffee. The inspector asked for a can of Coke. She not only brought an unopened can of Coke, but also dropped it when reaching over his shoulder. It struck the sharp edge of a radio control knob and which punctured the can. We had a spinning, fizzing, spraying Coke can decorating all of us and the cockpit with sticky stuff. I'd inadvertently disconnected the autopilot (somehow) and the airplane climbed 300 feet before it was recognized.

I said, "I presume you'll forgive that 300-foot deviation."

He replied, "I'd have given you 500 feet-plus with that chaos."

There was always (sadly) a well-defined relationship between one's Aeromedical Examiner and one's 'real doctor.' Rather a 'me against them' deal, every six months it was "You bet your job." ("How you been feeling?" "Fantastic. Sleep like a baby, never had a cold, nothing but peace and serenity in my life.")

One Kansas City AME passed away and a general aviation pilot had to find a new one.

"Let's read the eye chart. One eye at a time."

Now track this: The candidate put his right hand over his *right* eye and read it perfectly.

"Now the other eye."

Pilot-person put his left hand over his *right* eye and performed splendidly.

The doctor had to think a minute, but was rather confident he's been scammed.

"Okay. Let's put your right hand over your right eye, then your LEFT hand over your LEFT eye and do it again."

"Aw, hell, doc. I've been blind in that right eye for twenty years. No other AME ever caught that little charade."

My last comments to student pilots departing on their first solo cross-country trip was, "Remember. If you're lost, scared, or lonely, just dial in 121.5 (the emergency frequency) and bellow: HOWDY! You'll get all the attention, assistance or companionship you'll ever need."

Radio transmissions were always intimidating to student pilots. They knew the whole world was listening (not just one controller with a headset). Who hasn't transmitted, "Cessna Tower, this is Municipal 2368-Echo...damnit."

As I explained to one student: "A radio message is very simple. Who are you-Where are you-What do you want to do?" That's the way it was delivered: "Municipal Tower, Cessna 27020, Who am I, Where am I, and What do I want to do?" I think he replied, "*Wherever* you are, I think you *want* to talk to your instructor."

Rod Machado always advised his students: "In the event you make an off-airport landing, exit the airplane, get far from it in the event of fire, and then concentrate on erasing my name from every line in your logbook."

Another professional (and fantastic) aviation humor speaker, always in demand, is my friend Ralph Hood (www.ralphhood.com). Since Ralph is from Alabama, I always claimed his name was Joe-Bob Ralphus and he spoke Alabonics. While it contains not the least bit of truth, I told an audience that Ralph called me upon purchasing his first computer. He was unable to log on to the Internet. We spent a great deal of time talking about configuration and options, all of which Ralph claimed he didn't have. Finally I said, "WHAT KIND of computer do you have?"

He replied, "An E-6-B." (If Ralph's and Rod's humor tapes are not part of your collection, you're missing an evening of laughter.)

It didn't happen on my airport, but apparently happened elsewhere. One of the attempted tricks of 'experience' is called P-51 (Parker Pen-51) time in a logbook to falsify the amount of flight time. Ready for his checkride, but absent the required hours the checkride candidate noticed a plane on the ramp: N12345. He wrote in a large quantity of time that he had piloted N12345.

Upon presenting his logbook to the FAA Examiner, the latter remarked, "That N12345 is a nice airplane."

"Sure is," replied the candidate.

"I don't suppose you know that I own that airplane?" as he motioned out the window where it was parked.

The worst ATC transmission any pilot can hear is, "Contact the tower when you get down." My friends, that is simply handled: Don't come down!

Aw, you flooded the engines!

FAA RULE, NEW, MARK II, MOD 6
NOTICE OF PROPOSED RULEMAKING (NPRM)
Part 0, Section 000 (a) 1 (c)

Section I – No pilot or pilots, or person or persons acting on the direction or suggestion or supervision of a pilot or pilots, may try, or attempt to try or make, or make attempt to try to comprehend or understand any or all, in whole or in part of the herein mentioned Aviation Regulations, except as authorized by the Administrator or an agent appointed by, or inspected by, the Administrator. Section II – If a pilot, or group of associate pilots, becomes aware of, or realizes, or detects, or discovers, or finds that he or she, or they, are or have been beginning to understand the Aviation Regulations, they must immediately, within three (3) days notify, in writing, the Administrator.

Section III – Upon receipt of the above-mentioned notice of impending comprehension, the Administrator shall immediately rewrite the Aviation Regulations in such a manner as to eliminate any further comprehension hazards.

Section IV – The Administrator may, at his or her discretion, require the offending pilot or pilots to attend remedial instruction in Aviation Regulations until such time that the pilot is too confused to be capable of understanding anything.

THE TONGUE-IN-CHEEK CHECKRIDE
AS PUBLISHED IN *PLANE & PILOT* MAGAZINE (2003)

M any years ago I was asked about *attitude* in taking one's first check ride: the dreaded Private Pilot certification. I addressed this a long time ago and have been asked to repeat it. An upcoming first checkride certainly guarantees your apprehension, permeated with uncertainty and a jog into the jaws of judgment. Every student pilot is entitled to be armed with tactics and perspective to cope in this contest. Consider the first effort as *experience.*

Yes, you are expected to arrive two hours early, timid and insecure. Don't. You arrive late wearing reflective sunglasses that you do not remove. A long flowing scarf also creates an image. Flip your logbook and test validation on the desk, remarking, "Any score above 70 is overkill. Who needs it?" Your feet on the examiner's desk reflect your confidence. Look with obvious pride at your watch, then the examiner's watch and shake your head with disdain.

You are not a fawn caught in headlights. This is a personality contest to control the situation. After all, you are seeking to be a *pilot-in-command.* Politely ask the examiner, "Do you mind if I review your logbook, licenses and medical certificate as well?" He'll turn crimson and then you add, "I guess asking you to take a random drug test is out of the question?"

Expect a challenging oral exam. Whatever is asked, however, you reply, "My instructor said that wasn't important," or "My instructor said you'd ask some insignificant question like that. Can we move on to more important material?" Navigation problem? "I only fly locally." Keep the mood light. If you're asked what turns the airplane, your answer is: "The Creator, the ailerons are a signal to Heaven." Regulations? "All immaterial. I am the final authority on the operation of that airplane, allowed to deviate from any regulation to the extent required depending upon the conditions. I'll be the judge of that, thank you."

The airplane is the competitive platform, of course. If you've made it this far, first lead the examiner toward any World War II fighter than you might find parked on the ramp, then deviate to your own craft. Ask the examiner to check the fuel or the oil. "I just wanted to speed this up. I'll check it. You get the tie-downs." Once in the plane you remark, "I'll fly the airplane, you handle the radios." Another eruption. "OK, I'll do it all. What I suggested was good cockpit resource management, but I'll conduct this flight in whatever slipshod way you want." One should exert all the command authority possible.

Be cool at all times: "Aerial control, you authoritative glass-shrouded dudes, this bird needs to boogie to the cement and leap airborne." Never *Roger*: "10-4, big guy!" Get on the left brake, spin 360 with lots of power before taxi: "Just checking the area. Safety first." Also don't hesitate to say, "I'm the pilot. You touch anything and I'll break your fingers."

Airborne is the battlefield. Straight and level flight? "Which one do you want first?" Soon the examiner will ask for a takeoff and departure stall. "Stall? You want a stall? I don't do stalls. On takeoff I rotate at the top of the green arc and on landing I fly at the top of the white arc."

Nonetheless you'll be required to perform a full-power stall. You pull that puppy snappily up to 30 degrees of pitch, let it stall viciously and exclaim, "You've got it!" After the Fed fights for control, you clarify the situation: "You asked for a stall, not a recovery. Wasn't *that* a dandy?" Our companion will need a paper bag about now. Explain hyperventilation.

There are minor observations to inject during the flight at the right time: "*Some* wannabe pilots are so excitable that they shouldn't fly. No names mentioned." Or "I had a passenger last week as hyper as you." Another: "My instructor said you were a real horse's patoot. Personally I think you're a nice guy." ("Wanna buzz your house?" is not advised.)

Slow flight? "We just stalled it. Came down vertically. That's about as slow as we can get!" Steep turns? "I'd rather do a wing-over. It's more challenging. By the way, you ever do a loop in a Cessna? Wanna see one?"

Somewhere in this flight an engine is going to fail. The examiner will be distracted feeling for the fuel control selector on the floor. You, of course, have Super-Glued it in the ON position. With the distraction, dial in the emergency frequency (121.5) and then turn OFF the radio.

When the engine falters, grab the microphone and scream: "Mayday-Mayday-Mayday! Engine failure! Emergency!" You'll want to courteously offer another paper bag. It's also remotely possible that you'll be returning to your field of origin about now. In fact, the examiner may offer to fly the airplane. Maybe not.

In the pattern if you're high, you comment, "Yes, but I'm fast enough to handle it." If otherwise, you'll remark, "Yes, I'm quite low, but I'm also really slow enough to cope." Touchdown! Slam on those brakes! Put that examiner on the glare shield, maximum extension of the seatbelts. "I always test my brakes. You never know when you'll need all the efficiency possible."

In your mind this is wholly a test run. Examining the examiner. You'll relish in expressing a closing comment: "My last pink slip was a lot more neat than this one." And as you leave, do put your head around the doorframe to comment: "I suspected you'd get this upset. I'm glad I didn't use my own name, logbook and paperwork. Have you ever considered stress therapy?"

That's my advice. Try it. I've always wondered if it would work or how long that checkride would last.

A great flight always ends with a good landing:

Obviously someone had fun with PhotoPaint!

A Tribute to 'High Flight': An Immortal Poem

Two works originally grasping the beauty of flight were the novels of Antoine De Saint-Exupery ("St. X") and the marvelous poem of British Flight Lieutenant John Gillespie Magee, Jr. (1922-1941), who wrote the memorable "High Flight." St. X wrote: "Whether we call it sacrifice, or poetry or adventure, it is always the same voice that calls." From Flight we "...slipped the surly bonds of earth" and ultimately "...touched the face of God."

The creativity of pilots, monitored by the FAA, could not leave "High Flight" without amendment (and apology to Lt. Magee):

HIGH FLIGHT
Oh, I have slipped the surly bonds of earth[1],
And danced[2] the skies of laughter-silvered wings;
Sunward I've climbed[3] and joined the tumbling mirth[4]
Of sun-split clouds[5] and done a hundred things[6]
You have not dreamed of....Wheeled and soared and flung[7]
High in the sunlit silence[8]
Hov'ring there[9] I've chased the shouting wind[10] along and
    flung[11]
My eager craft through footless hall of air.
Up, up the long delirious[12],

Burning blue I've topped the wind-swept heights[13] with easy grace,
Where never lark, or even eagle[14] flew;
And while with silent, lifting mind
I've trod the high untrespassed sanctity of space[15]
Put out my hand[16] and touched the face of God.

NOTE:

1. Pilots must insure that all surly bonds have been slipped entirely before aircraft taxi or flight is attempted.
2. During periods of severe sky dancing, crew and passengers must keep seatbelts fastened. Crew should wear shoulder belts as well.
3. Sunward climbs must not exceed the maximum permitted aircraft ceiling.
4. Passenger aircraft are prohibited from joining the tumbling mirth.
5. Pilots flying through sun-split clouds under VFR (Visual Flight Rules) conditions must comply with all applicable minimum clearances.
6. Do not perform these hundred things in front of FAA inspectors.
7. Wheeling, soaring and swinging will not be attempted except in aircraft certified for such activities and within utility class weight limits.
8. Be advised that sunlit silence will occur only when a major engine malfunction has occurred.
9. 'Hov'ring there' will constitute a highly reliable signal that a flight emergency is imminent.

---

10. Forecasts of shouting winds are available from the local FSS (Flight Service Station). Encounters with unexpected shouting winds should be reported by pilots.

11. Pilots flinging eager aircraft through footless halls of air are reminded that they alone are responsible for maintaining separation from other eager craft.

12. Should any crewmember or passenger experience delirium while in the burning blue, submit an irregularity report upon flight termination.

13. Windswept heights will be topped by a minimum of 1000 feet to maintain VFR minimum separation.

14. Aircraft engines' ingestion of, or impact with, larks or eagles should be reported to the FAA and the appropriate aircraft maintenance facility.

15. Aircraft operating in the high untrespassed sanctity of space must remain in IFR flight regardless of meteorological conditions and visibility.

16. Pilots and passengers are reminded that opening doors or windows in order to touch the face of God may result in loss of cabin pressure.

LOW FLIGHT (For our helicopter readers)

Oh! I've slipped through the swirling clouds of dust,
And hovered out of ground effect on semi-rigid blades;
Earthward I've auto'ed and met the rising brush of non-paved terrain;
And done a thousand things you would never care to;
Skidded and dropped and flared low in the heat soaked roar.
Confined there, I've chased the earthbound traffic

And lost the race to insignificant headwinds;
Forward and up a little in ground effect I've topped a hedge
Where never Skyhawk and even Phantom flew.
Shaking and pulling collective,
I've lumbered the low untrespassed halls of Victor airways,
Put out my hand and touched a tree.

THE GREATEST LIES IN AVIATION

I'm from the FAA and I'm here to help you.

Me? I've never busted minimums.

I have no interest in flying for the airlines.

I fixed it right the first time. It must have failed for another reason.

I'm a member of the Mile High Club.

All that turbulence spoiled my good landing.

I only need glasses for reading.

Don't worry about the weight and balance. Airplanes can't read. It'll fly.

It flew in here; it'll fly out.

No need to look that up, I've got it memorized.

This airplane will out-perform the book by 20% or better.

Sure I can fly it! It's got wings, don't it?

I'm 22 years old, got 6000 hours, a four-year degree and 3000 hours in a Lear Jet.

In aviation we're overpaid, underworked and well-respected.

I have 5000 hours total time; 3200 are in actual instrument conditions.

I'm always glad to see the FAA!

We fly every day. We don't need any recurrent training.

It just came out of an annual inspection. How could anything be wrong?

I thought YOU took care of that.

Of course I know where we are.

I'm SURE the gear was down and checked.

And the best one ever spoken:

"There I was at forty thousand feet when the autopilot jumped out with the only parachute and left me with nothing except a silkworm and a sewing kit."

THE BETTER AVIATION JOKES

This may even have been a truthful recounting of an announcement:

A plane was at cruise and the Captain began his PA announcement: "Ladies and gentlemen, this is your captain. Welcome to Flight 223, nonstop from New York to Los Angeles. The weather ahead is good and we should have a smooth and uneventful flight. Now sit back, relax and…OH MY GOD!!!"

The cabin silence was interrupted only by pounding hearts. The captain came back on the PA: "I'm sorry to have startled you. Our flight attendant bought me a cup of coffee and spilled hot coffee in my lap. You should see the front of my pants."

One passenger quipped, "He should see the back of mine!"

━━━

It is well-known that God created the airline captain because He Himself could not be everywhere.

━━━

How many airline pilots does it take to screw in a light bulb? Just one to hold it because the entire world revolves around him.

━━━

The young flight attendant asked the more aged captain, "When was the last time you ever made love?"

He replied, "Oh, about nineteen-fifty-five."

"Wow…it's been that long?"

He looked at his watch and said, "Well, hell, it's only twenty-one hundred hours now."

Two flight attendants were walking down a country road and encountered a frog. "Kiss me," begged the frog, "and I'll turn into a handsome airline captain." They both laughed and continued walking. One turned, went back to pick up the frog and placed it in her jacket pocket.

"Are you really going to kiss that frog?" asked her friend.

"Oh Lord, NO!" she replied. "But do you know how much more money I can get for a talking frog than I can get for an airline captain?"

The second punchline to that story is, "Kiss me, I'll marry you and you can clean my home, do my laundry and make love to me on demand." The flight attendant hastened to acquire the frog and that night she had frog legs for dinner.

The passenger boarded the airplane wearing a red suit, red shirt, red tie and with two small horns on his head.

"You're in seat 6-A," stated the flight attendant, looking at the boarding pass.

"I'm the devil, you know."

"Yes, I can see that. You're in seat 6-A."

Touring the cabin before takeoff she instructed, "Buckle your seatbelt."

"I'm the devil, you know."

"Yes, I know that. Now buckle your seatbelt."

"Bring me a drink."

She sighed, "We'll serve drinks when we're airborne."

"Obviously you don't know who I am!"

"Yes, I do," she replied.

"Aren't you intimidated by that?"

"Look I've got two guys up front and they both know they're God. You're no competition."

———

There was the passenger who asked for a cup of coffee as they were boarding. "I'm sorry, sir, but we'll be serving coffee after we're airborne."

"Well," he huffed. "If you were a guest in *my* house and wanted a cup of coffee, I'd see that you had one promptly."

She smiled, "Yes, I'm sure you would. And if I were a guest in your house I would not bring two hundred friends with me."

———

At the ticket counter the well-dressed businessman asked to buy a round-trip ticket. "To where?" inquired the agent.

"To right back here, of course," he replied.

———

Our Airline Pilots Association was always accused of demanding unreasonable wages and working conditions. This gave birth to the story of the local union meeting. The chairman rose to announce, "We've reached the conclusion that our goals and necessary quality of living will be met by shutting down this airline to one day a week. We'll all fly turnaround trips, out and back, home every night. That day will be Wednesday. Is there any discussion?"

From the rear one senior captain leaped to his feet, "Now just a minute! Are you talking about *every* damned Wednesday?!?"

———

Approaching Columbus, Ohio's municipal airport crosses the golf course on the east end of the field, the captain transmitted, "Well, it looks like all the controllers are out on the golf course today."

"Yes, sir," replied the tower. "They are all caddies for the airline pilots."

———

There's no creativity or black humor as gets born in an airline ramp office. With the tragedy of Waco, Texas, it was apparent that David Koresh had a big house, lots of money, many women, loved sex, had a lot of children and thought he was God. Therefore, it was concluded that Koresh was an American Airlines captain.

———

In that same vein someone posted the news article about the Eastern Airlines captain who had killed his wife, froze the body and disposed of it through a wood-chipper. Beneath the article someone wrote: "Shape up or chip out!"

———

The flight attendant asked the passenger for his boarding pass. He in turn opened a trench coat and flashed her. "Sir, I asked for your boarding pass, not your stub."

You always know when you've invited airline crews over for dinner. When the meal is complete, the pilots will put their plates on the floor and the flight attendants will wipe their hands on the curtains. (Maybe you have to be 'airline' to get that one.)

En route to Las Vegas a gentleman was seated beside a gorgeous lady in First Class. Anxious to meet her and possibly romance her later, he inquired about the purpose for her trip.

"I'm attending a convention."

"Interesting. What convention is it?"

"It's for members of the Free Love Society."

He is now desperately interested in this lovely hunk of fluff.

"Tell me," he asked, "in your obvious and vast experience, what men are the best lovers?"

"First," she replied, "I'd have to say airline pilots. They are commanding, impressive with all that gold and glitter on uniforms, and confident men. Next the American Indian, that sense of ancient savagery, the essence of the warring brave is quite exotic. Then perhaps the Jewish gentleman. They patronize their women, buy them gifts and place them on a pedestal."

"Interesting," he exclaimed. "Allow me to introduce myself. I'm Captain Tonto Goldberg."

A small boy followed an immensely large woman, weaving her way down the aisle. She was three times the lad's size in height and width. Her beeper sounded. "Daddy, let's move. I think she's backing up."

═══

Two hunters seeking elk in Canada had chartered a seaplane. Upon its arrival, the young pilot looked at the supplies that would be a challenge to a C-5A and said, "No way. There's no way we can take that much gear in this airplane."

"Well," snarled one of the hunters, "this is exactly what we brought last year without a problem. Maybe he was just a better pilot than you."

That did it! The young aviator lifted, loaded, crammed, stuffed and actually got all that equipment into a plane now floating with submerged pontoons.

He applied power, circled the lake…circled three more times trying to gain airspeed (hence, lift), finally got it on the step and trimmed a tree getting airborne. Relief!

Three days later the pilot arrived to retrieve the hunters. They now have the equipment and two elk.

"No way. There is NO way I can carry all the equipment, the two of you and two full-grown ELK, fercryingoutloud."

"Well," spoke one. "LAST YEAR we did this. We had all of this, two elk, and the pilot didn't complain. Maybe he was just a better pilot than you are."

That did it! He lifted, loaded, crammed, stuffed and got an elk in the cargo compartment. One elk to go.

"Well, LAST YEAR that outstanding pilot tied the elk around the fuselage just aft of the wing. HE knew what he was doing and was, of course, a superb pilot.

That did it!

They circled the lake twenty times, airspeed building, floats surfacing from five feet below the surface, flying speed a possibility, and finally, lift off!

They hit the trees at about thirty feet of altitude. A plane, people, cargo and elks decorated the terrain in a fifty yard pattern.

As one hunter regained consciousness, he moaned, "Where are we?"

The other whispered, "About twenty yards farther than we got last year."

═══

A new mother boarded the aircraft with her little infant. She found her seat, cuddled the child and uncovered the baby's head.

Her seatmate commented, "That's the ugliest baby I've ever seen. It looks like a monkey!"

She is immediately upset, insulted and crying. The flight attendant heard her distress and hastened to her aid. "Ma'am, I sorry you're upset. Can I get you some coffee, tea or a soft drink…and perhaps a banana for your monkey?"

═══

A husband suspects his wife is having an affair with the airline pilot who lives next door. Finally her challenges her directly.

Her reply, "If I've told you once, I've told you niner-thousand times, *negative* on the affair!"

═══

Old and still good: Decorated WWII fighter pilot Ole Olson was describing aerial combat at an aviation banquet: "We had these fokkers coming at us from all directions. I shot down one fokker, my wing man shot down two of them fokkers and together we took all of those fokkers out of the air."

The somewhat aggrieved Master of Ceremonies hastened to say: "A fascinating story. Of course we all know that the Fokker was a World War Two German fighter airplane."

"Ya," said Ole, "but THESE fokkers were Messerschmidts."

How does a young lady know when her date with a pilot reaches the midway point?

When he says, "That's enough about flying. Let's talk about me."

What's the difference between a pilot and a pig?

"In any bar when a pig gets drunk it doesn't try picking up a pilot."

Boeing will introduce the Boeing 747-600, all automated with a crew of two: a pilot and a Doberman. The pilot is there to feed the dog and the dog is there to attack the pilot if he tries to touch anything.

A young pilot took his girl to the airport and was expounding on his flight progress in a (Cessna) C-150.

She's clueless, of course, so asks, "How big is a C-150?" He noted a USAF cargo plane on the ramp and said: "Well, THAT is a C-130."

≡≡≡

When Cessna entered the jet market, they produced the first Cessna Citation. It was a splendid airplane which did what it was designed to do: operate economically, relatively short range, certified for single-pilot operation, superb short-field capabilities, straight-wing design and flight plans were filed in knots rather than Mach numbers. Of course the high performance, high speed and high altitude pilots couldn't resist needling a Citation I driver:

"The Citation has a screen over the engine exits, so they won't ingest fast-flying birds." (The jokes stopped with the later series, and the Citation X meets any competition.)

Sometimes It *Does* Take A Rocket Scientist!
(Purely A Rumor)

Scientists at NASA built a gun specifically to launch dead chickens at the windshields of airliners, military jets and the space shuttle, all traveling at maximum velocity. The idea is to simulate the frequent incidents of collisions with airborne fowl to test the strength of the windshields. British engineers heard about the gun and were eager to test it on the windshields of their new high speed trains.

Arrangements were made and a gun was sent to the British engineers. When the gun was fired, the engineers stood shocked as the chicken hurled out of the barrel, crashed into the shatterproof shield, smashed it to smithereens, blasted through the control console, snapped the engineer's back-rest in two, and embedded itself in the back wall of the cabin, like an arrow shot from a bow.

The horrified Brits sent NASA the disastrous results of the experiment, along with the designs of the windshield and begged the U.S. scientists for suggestions.

(You're going to love this…)

NASA responded with a one-line memo: "Defrost the chicken."

AIRPLANES VS. WOMEN

Airplanes can kill you quickly; a woman takes her time.
Airplanes can be turned on by the flick of a switch
Airplanes don't get mad if you "touch and go."
Airplanes don't object to a preflight inspection.
Airplanes come with a manual to explain their operation.
Airplanes have a strict weight-and-balance limit
Airplanes can be flown any day of the month.
Airplanes don't come with in-laws.
Airplanes don't care how many other airplanes you've
flown.
Airplanes and pilots both arrive at the same time.
Airplanes don't mind if you look at other airplanes.
Airplanes don't mind if you buy airplane magazines.
Airplanes expect to be tied down.
Airplanes don't comment on your piloting skills
Airplanes don't whine unless something is really wrong.
BUT, when airplanes get real quiet, just like a woman,
something is really, *really* wrong.

Signs You've Chosen a "No Frills" Airline

They don't sell tickets, they sell chances.

All the insurance machines in the terminal are sold out.

Before the flight, the passengers get together and elect a pilot.

You cannot board the plane unless you have the exact change.

Before you took off, the stewardess tells you to fasten your Velcro.

The Captain asks all the passengers to chip in a little for gas.

When they pull the steps away, the plane starts rocking.

The Captain yells at the ground crew to get the cows off the runway.

You ask the Captain how often their planes crash and he says, "Just once."

No movie. Don't need one. Your life keeps flashing before your eyes.

You see a man with a gun, but he's demanding to be let off the plane.

All the planes have both a bathroom and a chapel.

MEMORIES

Many years ago we had an inmate riot at the state prison in close-by Leavenworth, Kansas. A television station sent a camera-armed reporter to videotape the scene. One thing any helicopter pilot learns quickly is that a photographer (still or videotape) can never get low enough or close enough. One does not take directions from them without considering every specific of any request. An example:

Reporter: "How about you fly us to hover right on top the prison wall so I can get some shots inside the prison?"

Me: "How about we get shot down by the guards who think we're there to help a prisoner escape? This is as close as you're getting."

━━━

We had a contract to fly oil-conveying-transfer pipelines at low altitude in helicopters. At low flight we could see any breakage by discoloration of the land or discover anyone drilling or building above the submerged oil lines (very big and at high pressure). We'd fly a well-marked route, which was clear of trees and structures. One day I invited a friend to fly with me (although not authorized to do so).

Kansas had a lengthy drought. We flew by a large lake, now shrunk 75% by evaporation. A virtual tidal wave was observed within it. As I returned it was actually disturbance from fish! There were hundreds and barely submerged in the extremely low water level. They were dashing from one side to the other with the audible presence of the helicopter and the downwash disturbance. Hey, I thought, "Let's spear one of them!"

I landed the helicopter. We found a small tree, cut it, pruned it and fashioned a spear point on one end. "Now I'll hover over the lake and you carefully, SLOWLY, step out on the skid and spear one of those critters. What a laugh it'll be to bring it back."

He was neither careful nor slow! A lightweight observation Hughes 300 is quite sensitive in the lateral axis. Almost immediately I was swinging the cyclic from left to right trying to offset the passenger's weight and didn't intend for him to be FULLY on the skid (only one foot was intended).

The fisherman, in turn, is trying to cling to this gyrating platform, which then flipped him off the skid and into the lake. He was drenched, then standing in knee-deep water, feet at least one foot invested in mud.

I motioned for him to grab a skid, lifted him sufficiently to drag his body to the edge and then landed. "You're a MESS! Get in and we'll fly to some small airport and clean out this helicopter!" Returning to our airport, he sat on a canvas tarp we'd borrowed.

Conclusion: Carry a harpoon. Carry a gun. Throw spears. DO NOT ever attempt to hand-spear fish from a lightweight helicopter.

For the instructor's rating in gliders (sailplanes) one must demonstrate two different kinds of tows to get aloft during the checkride. Of course we had the airplane that hauled us upward during training, but had to design some kind of a second tow: bungee cord or auto-tow. The first wasn't even obtainable. We set up a tractor with a winch, got a very long nylon cord and tied it to a car. The car began to accelerate from one end of the field, pulling the glider to flying speed from the other. It was touchy! In fact, all we gained was minimum altitude, barely enough to complete the pattern and land at the other end. And…if you delayed the 'release' you might pitch nose-down, following the line to the tractor!

We were three candidates. I was first. The FAA Examiner stated, "I'm not going to ride in that. You do a right pattern, land, and the rating ride is over." No one considered that turning right was downwind. I was carried a startling distance from the airport. In fact, the only way to return was to fly directly to the end of the runway and virtually do an aerobatic wingover to reverse course and be aligned with the runway.

That particular airport was on a slight hill. From the far end you could not see the other. All they saw was a wingover maneuvered glider, nose down, which disappeared from sight.

As everyone crested the hill in a dead run, they saw a glider on the runway, all windows steamed by the perspiration of the pilot. "Maybe we'd better turn left after the release from the tow."

Stupid is as Stupid Does

Once in the 1970s I ferried a helicopter from Orange County, California back to Kansas City. It was purchased by the police department and was mandated to have 25 hours on the machine for their acceptance. Orange County was the home of TallMantz Aviation. I accepted the helicopter from the movieland-famous Frank Tallman, the pilot in such great films such as "Mad-Mad-Mad World," where he flew through the billboard. "Only it was supposed to be one-quarter-inch or less plywood. They used three-quarter-inch and it virtually destroyed the airplane." Paul Mantz had been killed in the movie "Flight of the Phoenix" when the airplane disintegrated upon landing. Paul had been an advisor to Amelia Earhart in her around-the-world efforts. Frank Tallman was later killed in a Cessna 310, scouting out filming sites. What a humble, gracious gentleman and host was that great pilot.

All of my rotorcraft time had been in the Midwest, low terrain and moderate temperatures. The plan was to fly it across the desert, NO radios and two five-gallon gas cans to refuel when need be. Also, the flight plan was to fly the Southern Route around the Rockies, since the machine didn't have the performance to cross at Denver or that region. So the route to come home would be from southern Texas.

Arriving at airports of 5000-plus foot altitudes on 100-degree days, it was a density altitude education. Once was hanging 20 feet above the field, rotor blades bent upward, and I couldn't land or fly. Couldn't release pitch for RPM or it fell. Couldn't get RPM with the blades 'bent' upward.

It became obvious: redline the rotor RPM in high-density altitude airports. Anywhere in the green arc was adequate in Kansas. That's not the story.

Arriving in New Mexico at twilight (and having learned you do not wear shorts in a Plexiglas cockpit on hot sunny days, thereby sunburned to misery), I landed. The hotel had been notified to pick me up about that time.

An elderly gentleman approached the helicopter and said, "I've never been up in one of these. I'd sure like to. What would you charge me for a short ride?"

I said, "I have to put 25 hours or more on the helicopter and may not. Jump in and I'll just give you a ride."

So we hovered, did tail-rotor turns around a point, some quick-stop exercises to hover and once around the pattern. He was thrilled.

I came down for dinner, sunburned, exhausted, dehydrated, so very hungry. The waitress placed a pitcher in front of me: "This is a pitcher of martinis. The boss was so grateful for the ride that you can have all you want."

The next morning, if I had opened my eyes I'd have bled to death. Martini sick (hangover) beyond description. Additionally, the police department had ordered floats on the helicopter. All day long I had to release air with the expansion by the heat. This morning they were crumpled and deflated by the cool of night. I was on my knees blowing up the floats to some level, else they would fold under the helicopter in flight. Of course all the airport occupants in New Mexico were entertained by anyone with floats, and especially this guy performing an apparent obscene act on them.

The day was terribly gusty. The route was the Guadalupe Pass, all mountains. With one gust, a blade went out of phase: Whirl-whirl-WOMP. It was so hot, so gusty, such a jarring ride in mountainous terrain and with a raging martini hangover. My thoughts were simple: "I could die, but I'll bet I'm not going to be lucky enough for that to happen." Eighty, eighty-five miles an hour, California to Kansas, via Southern Texas: Never again.

It was fun to track the Kansas Turnpike at sunset. The shadow of the helicopter was far in front of me. I'd parallel the turnpike, then drop the shadow in front of cars and watch them slam on the brakes. Great fun.

I did, however, always stop where fuel was inexpensive:

I Remember Al

I always claimed to have learned to fly on a small field. In fact we had Runway 23-33. You had to be talented to navigate that elbow. That's not really true about me or the airport. Al Wilson gave me my first job in aviation as his General Manager.

Al Wilson founded Wilson Flight Training Center, Fairfax Airport (now gone) in Kansas City. It was a 400-plus student, 43-airplane training facility. He was a legend in K.C. aviation, and one of the finest educators in the industry. In 1977, he was lost in a Beechcraft Debonair accident in Ft. Myers, Florida, for reasons never determined.

Al told me about the early days of his own flight training: open cockpit aircraft with virtually no communication between the two cockpits other than a tube into which you could yell. There was one instructor who had a dramatic means to transfer control, virtually 'solo' the student. He would disconnect his own control stick and tap the student on the shoulder. Once the student's attention was gained and he turned to see the instructor in the aft cockpit, the latter would display the disconnected control stick and pitch it overboard. Wow…the student was on his own, no one to salvage anything into which he might blunder.

Al had heard of this practice and had a good sense of humor himself. He found and hid in the airplane a *second* control stick in the forward cockpit. When the instructor tapped him on the shoulder, Al turned and watched the control stick fly overboard. Al nodded vigorously and then (apparently*) threw his own control stick overboard.*

Back on the ground he said the instructor ripped him up one side and the other, but gave up that instructional technique.

———

Al was a pipe smoker. He was always filling, lighting, tapping, cleaning and puffing that pipe. I learned whatever patience I have from Al. It drove me to internal turmoil in a meeting when one sentence was interrupted five times: filling, lighting, tapping, cleaning and puffing. That's part of the story.

One of my dearest friends "Mac" (Uncle Mac to my daughter) had an unwired oil plug fall from the Cessna 150 on a training flight. Oil pressure fell immediately with instant oil drainage. He landed splendidly in a bean field. Al and I drove to the scene (in separate cars) to see the airplane and assess the damage to it and the property. Our mechanic put in a new plug, started the airplane, and declared that he believed no damage had been done by Mac's fast action in noting the oil pressure loss and shutting down the engine.

At the end of the field were high telephone wires. I said, "Al, I can fly that plane out of here."

He was livid. "Do you see those wires?"

I said, "Yes, and if I can't go over them, I'll go under them. I can fly this airplane out of here."

He was absolutely distraught with me. "I am not going to sacrifice a $20,000 airplane or you because you THINK you can fly it out of here. Now let's get a trailer, get the wings off of it and I'll tow it back to the airport."

I left while he and Jack, the mechanic, disassembled the airplane, got it on the trailer and he began to drive the thirty-plus miles back to Fairfax Airport. Of course he was filling, lighting, tapping (out the window), cleaning and puffing.

Another car pulled alongside him and the passengers were frantically signaling his attention to the load he was towing. The airplane was burning. He'd tapped ashes out the window and ignited whatever fuel was dripping from the disconnected wings.

It was the closest he ever came to genuine anger with me (and as close to firing me) when I was hysterical with laughter as he arrived at the flight school, towing a blackened skeleton of a Cessna 150. "Damn, Al. I'm glad we didn't risk that airplane by letting me fly it out of there!" Livid is an understatement.

It was at Wilson Flight Training Center that we originated the "Self Solo Program," although we didn't know it. Each instructor was assigned one of the many airplanes, specifically the fully instrument-equipped airplanes for full versatility of training all students. We hired only our own graduated students as instructors, all Instrument instructors as well as basic licensing. There was, therefore, a column on the schedule for the instructor and one for 'his' airplane. The student's name would appear in both columns: Instructor and Airplane. If the instructor was off, his column was blank and the airplane was available to any student (or part-time instructor).

As an instructor I had often said, "I could teach a monkey to takeoff and land an airplane, but I can never teach him to *think!* That is the measure of a pilot." You never know when you've enrolled a contestant for that philosophical position.

An instructor called in sick. The scheduler erased his schedule, but failed to erase the same student's name under his assigned aircraft. He of great courage and/or consummate stupidity arrived for his lesson. He saw that he was not scheduled with an instructor, but did see his name under the airplane column. There can be only one conclusion: "This is the day he wants me to solo." Six hours flight time!

I got a call from the control tower: "We've got a real problem here. One of your airplanes has made about six passes at one landing. He's all over the place and he sounds scared." I'll be right there! I rushed to the ramp and listened on the radio of a parked Cessna while senior instructor Bill Howell directed the student to MCI, then called Midcontinent International Airport. It was also only a long strip of cement and a temporary tower.

He was trying to get it on the ground. It took encouragement, calmness and some verbal instruction to talk him onto a final. When he was about twenty feet above the ground, Bill said, "Cut the engine. Put it down. Put it down anywhere. Leave it down." He bounced a few times, but came to a stop ON the runway with no damage to the Cessna.

In my office and learning the facts, I asked, "Wouldn't you think it was a poor flight school to not even notify you, brief you or supervise you on your first solo?" Well, he thought it was unusual, but he just wanted to do whatever his instructor expected of him. "Didn't it strike you as a fearful adventure with such limited time?"

"Well…yeah, I was scared, but I just wanted to do whatever my instructor wanted me to do."

I recall crossing my arms on the desk, putting my head down into them and saying, "Do not schedule or fly anything until you, your instructor and I have a meeting."

It was probably the first Self Solo Program in an FAA-Approved School.

━━━

I was in the tower one day visiting my controller pal, Bill Painter. Unknown to me, the manager of our competing flight school had also entered the tower and was standing to the back of it.

A hearse arrived. An airplane awaited it on the ramp. Transporting the deceased by airplane to a funeral location elsewhere was not unusual. What was unusual was they removed the sheet and the body was clearly exposed for them (and us) to maneuver it into the airplane.

I quipped, "What's going on? Did (competing) flight school solo another student?"

The competing manager stormed out of that tower and refused to speak for me for some length of time.

In memory: In 1974 we lost my daughter's beloved Uncle Mac in a crash of the twin-engine airplane in which I trained him and got him named on the insurance policy as an instructor. Mac did what I'd asked him never to do—a V_{mc} demonstration on a very hot day at low altitude. I've missed him every day of the last 28 years. I suspected what might happen, but a flat spin probability was never in the manual or any training bulletin.

There was even some amusement attached to that much later with all of its legal ramifications. *Many years later* an attorney arrived unexpectedly at TWA's training center asking for me. He wanted to solicit my testimony as an expert witness for the manufacturer in a twin engine accident in 1974. The scant details left no doubt what accident he was citing. I asked what was the premise of his client?

"We contend that it was a careless, reckless and inattentive instructor who was responsible for the accident and fatalities."

I replied, "You've overlooked two things: I trained that instructor, and he was one of my best friends."

The attorney muttered a bit and commented, "I don't guess there is anyway to keep you out of this?"

Not now, pal. I testified on behalf of Mac. His widow and the students received an abundant settlement.

THE TRAINING CENTER

I was privileged to teach in both classrooms and simulators within the airline's training center (707, 727, 767, Meteorology, Regulations, Radar). Like flight instructing, it was rewarding to me to impart knowledge and confidence to others. I have often quoted that dear, gentle man Richard Bach in speaking of *Jonathan Livingston Seagull*: "…he was born to be an instructor and his way of giving love was to give something that he'd learned for himself to a gull who asked to know." The training center was, however, fun-filled as well.

═══

For one Recurrent Training day a captain had flown the red-eye flight from LAX. He sat in the front row and was having exceptional difficulty staying awake. Soon all of us were watching his head bob downward and then snap up in waking. There was only one thing to do: talk more quietly and melodiously. I put him out! Then I motioned 'silence' to the class, 'get up' and 'out.' I had to teach for a few more minutes because the son of a gun almost woke up. Then I shut off the projector, turned off the lights in the room, and we all met at the coffee machine. In time he came tearing out of that room like a disoriented bull, not knowing where he was, what day it was or where he was supposed to be.

The director at the time regarded me as a thorn he had to bear. I was teaching too many classes to "send that rabble-rouser back to the line." On the 707 we had *seven* P-Panels (Power panels, Circuit breaker isolations). For reasons I never understood, except to demonstrate knowledge, a new engineer had to recite how to disable the entire power flow, one circuit breaker at a time. "P-2 feeds P-5; P-4 feeds P-2, etc." Only my powers of observation noted there were *seven* urinals in the men's room. With red ribbon and scotch tape, I turned them into an educational experience. A red ribbon ran from Pee-2 to Pee-5 and from Pee-4 to Pee-2. Yes, I did a rug dance, and yes, I was permitted to take them down.

—=—

I seemed to lock horns with him without intent. At an assembled meeting I made three bad mistakes. First mistake, my back was to the door of entry. I said, "When I was a boy it seemed grown-ups always had meetings and I wondered what they did." (Second mistake: No one asked and I continued.) "Now I'm grown up, we still have meetings and I *still* don't know what we do." (Third observation of mistake, no one laughed.) The voice behind me said, "You are now invited to leave this one, Mr. Gwinn." Yes, another rug dance.

—=—

Naval Aviator Charles Plumb was shot down over Viet Nam and spent a horribly abusive time as a POW. He wrote an inspirational book entitled *I'm No Hero,* although in the mind of everyone, he surely was. He is now a paid motivational speaker and superb!

Charlie Plumb was hired by TWA to videotape a motivational speech on acceptance and coping. The intent was to present it during Recurrent Training. First it was reviewed by the instructors, who were asked to comment on the presentation. Naturally everyone was awestruck and uplifted by this brave man's ordeal and strength of character.

Smiling as I composed it, my own evaluation read, "During this Icahn management of TWA, I can think of no more appropriate personality to discuss acceptance and optimism with us than a bona fide and fellow prisoner-of-war."

Yeah, another rug dance and my prose was trashed with venomous comment. There was just no place for creativity.

God bless Charlie Plumb, a brave man, a credit to our country.

Teaching the same class over and over can sometimes be boring. Such was the case with a Recurrent class, one that did not even require me to observe the slide being projected since I'd done it so often. We had rear projection from an isolated room. A slide stuck. I was miffed. I walked back, grabbed the lens, banged the projector and the slide dropped. The class continued. Another slide stuck, my abruptness with the projector was more harsh. Unknown to me, the heat lens broke. Slides behind me appeared and went *poof!* Instantly incinerated. That class allowed me to cremate about thirty slides before the first laughter began.

Full motion, visual simulators were splendid. As a new flight engineer instructor, I was still learning all the switches and selections to make things happen. I noticed the Emergency Power Off switch had indications on the knob that it rotated as one pushed it in. Did it really twist? I moved it about one-eighth of an inch and the entire operation slammed to a halt. The simulator fell into the jacks supporting it and I sat paralyzed. Naturally I was inquiring, trying to help the technicians find out what caused the fault. You can also bet I was so new to the operation that "I ain't admitting nuttin'." I think that simulator was down for about twelve hours. They never found the flaw, but got it operational. I was complimentary.

In the 727 simulator I was training another instructor. Everyone is seated, buckled in, except me. The computer decided to go bonkers (or 'tango uniform' as we might have said). First it rolled violently to the left and I bounced off that wall; then to the right as I ricocheted off another wall. It began to shudder, went totally black and slammed into the jacks with terrible impact. Everyone is stunned, hurt a bit and I'm lying bruised on the floor. In the utter darkness the first officer remarked, "Damn, I'd had that happen *in the airplane* a lot, but *never the simulator!*" We were howling in laughter and moaning simultaneously.

One Captain candidate was just a superb fellow, but he stuttered when he was really frustrated, only then. He was flying the simulator on an ILS approach, both needles looking like a sword-fight. Finally when he momentarily centered the glide slope, the instructor hit 'Altitude Hold' and winked at me. When the localizer needle was passing center (again!) the instructor pushed 'Position Hold.' One could observe the student begin to relax, shoulders drop, the comfort of good performance soothing the moment. Both needles centered and stabilized. He turned to us, smiled, and boasted, "F-F-F-Fat C-City."

======

When the Vice President of Flight Operations came to Recurrent Training, all the flags of attentiveness were run to the top of the flagpole. I was to teach the Flight Management Computer on the 767 in a one-hour refresher class. The Director (yes, he who disdained me) summoned me to say, "You are not to conduct this class differently from any other. From an educational viewpoint, this is just another Captain, and you present training as we normally would. Do you understand me?"

I entered the classroom for this *one-man class*, but didn't see the Director slip in the rear. My opening: "Gentlemen, this is Recurrent Training. I don't want to hear about your bids, your stock losses, your divorce or damned contract complaints. We're going to talk about the 767." The VP howled; the director fumed. Another rug dance. Always the same tune.

======

We did training for foreign carriers as well. One Middle Eastern group opened the door and it was irresistible. "Where do you find the women in this city?"

I said, "Well, most of the pilots find all the gals at the Esquire Club. I understand it's about a 4-to-1 ratio of good-looking chicks." Unfortunately I couldn't tell them where it was, but I remembered the phone number: "Just dial E-S-Q-U-I-R-E on your telephone and ask directions." (Try to find a "Q" on your telephone—t'ain't there.) Amazingly, no one confronted me or complained the next time we gathered.

We had one instructor who was a splendid gentleman with a soft monotone voice. He had splendid credentials and knew his subject, but unfortunately no one could stay awake with his sonorous voice. He was known as The Sandman. One day a captain in the back of the room began to snore loudly. The instructor was offended: "Someone wake up that man!"

A captain in the front row responded: "Hell, YOU put him to sleep; YOU wake him up."

We had a new Ground Instructor start at TWA at the same time I was hired. I was the only civilian pilot in a class of military/airline jet jockeys, seven Academy graduates and a gathering of intimidating contemporaries. We were working E6B computer problems. New himself and not all that comfortable, the new instructor began, "Let's compute the Mach (speed of sound) value of 220 knots, altitude is 35,000 feet and the outside air temp is minus-42 degrees." We spun computer wheels and someone would exclaim: "Mach point-8-4" or whatever the solution might have been.

As this progressed, the new instructor was gaining confidence, and he finally offered the real challenge: "All right, gentlemen, you're in the Apollo spacecraft, speed is 25,000 miles per hour, altitude is 200,000 feet and outside air temp is minus-150. Let's see if you can solve that one!"

Fifteen of us reached for computers as classmate John commented, "It's ZERO. You're in a vacuum." (Sound does not travel in a vacuum, therefore it could not be computed as a value.) The new instructor turned a bit red and recovered beautifully: "That's splendid thinking, John. I'm glad you got it."

===

My most memorable training center associate was a truly intelligent man, quite aggressive, a contemplative individual who seemed to have no neutrals in others' regard for him. Someone accused him of having no humility. He confided to me, "The people I meet who are the most humble have every damned reason to be."

His crowning glory of tactlessness was explained to me when he was simply puzzled by the discord at home after he had a meeting with his children. "I told them that I loved them, wanted only the best for them, hoped they found someone to love forever and had every success. My only advice for each of them was: Do not have children, because frankly none of you were worth the grief." He was baffled by my convulsing laughter. "I was just trying to help them have a good life, with plenty of funds and freedom. My wife is enraged!"

Then there was the old story of the captain who said he'd never marry again: "I'll just go out and find a woman who hates me and buy her a new house."

Another instructor received a call from his son in college who needed a large amount of money to buy the Izod Lacoste athletic shirts; they were the rage and sported the alligator stitched on the breast. "Well, son. I'll compromise. I'm sending you two dozen T-shirts and an alligator stamp. You make your own."

When TWA grounded all the DC-9s in the 70s, only to reacquire them later in another retreat from a bad decision, the DC-9 crews had been a virtual family. They all flew together out of Kansas City, were comfortable with the routes and each other, and deeply resented being forced to transition to the Boeing 727. One Captain was talking his oral quiz from the FAA toward the award of a 727-type rating. "What does this ground interconnect switch do, Captain?" Answer: It connects the B Hydraulic system to the A system for backup. "What does the Emergency Inflight Override Switch do?" Answer: It connects the B System to the A system for backup.

"What does the Brake Interconnect Switch do?" Answer: It connects the B System to the A System for backup. The FAA Examiner asked, "Now why would we have three switches that all do the same thing?" Reply: "I don't know and I don't give a damn. This is the most screwed-up airplane I ever flew." End of exam, a visit to the VP's office, and the next day he really, *really* cared about those system differences.

———

After I left the Training Center, it amused me to send pilot comments back to them on the sheet of paper for that purpose within the Recurrent Training bulletin. For those who may not know VASI (Visual Approach Slope Indicator), it is a landing aid with white and red lights. All red: too low. All white: too high. Red over white: on the proper descent path.

My message: "I think we should eliminate use of the VASI system from our Flight Operations and Policy Manual until the FAA standardizes it. It is too unpredictable. I've seen it all red and often all white. Sometimes it's red over white and I expect to see white over red at any time. Since we cannot rely on a system like this, why do we teach and use it?"

I received a phone call that night from my pal, the manager of Ground Training, to say, "I know you sent that report. I said not a word when the safety manager called in the Procedures instructor. They were reading the Aeronautical Information Manual attempting to reason out the logic of that pilot suggestion. Good show. Don't do it again."

That made it a dare, didn't it?

My next suggestion: "We are finding that first officers rotating to the line are well trained and competent aviators. But it's a given that any idiot can fly an airplane; it takes a genius to *bid* trips. Why aren't you allotting more time to

Bidding Procedures and Tactics instead of all this systems stuff?"

It was ignored. I didn't even get the courtesy of a phone call.

———

When Bob Dunham and I were contemporary flight instructors in the '60s, we never imagined we'd be contemporary TWA Captains in the '90s. And in a unique scheduling surprise, we were simulator partners both in upgrade to First Officer and then to Captain. We often had briefings at 0500 and left the hotel at 0430.

One weekend there was a big-big dog show held at that hotel. It was most enjoyable to me, a dog lover. It was irresistible to Bob, an opportunist. As we exited a long, ground-level corridor at 0430 for a simulator report, Bob paused and produced a shrieking, warbling whistle, commonly known as "Here, boy!" It sounded like 300 dogs made that effort, barking behind closed doors. We left, of course.

"I feel like we're missing something."

TRIBUTE TO PAUL

Paul was one of the finest ground instructors with whom I was privileged to work. Dedicated, thoroughly knowledgeable, a total gentleman and dedicated Christian. There continues a deep, genuine friendship and affection between us. That did not preclude 'the needle.'

Our manager had a rather unique way of greeting people: "How's Dave today?" I found it distancing, not a personable expression, and just didn't like it. I usually responded: "Oh, I don't know. If I see him, I'll ask." All Paul needed to know was *what irritated Dave.*

If I lifted my phone, there was a label under it: "How's Dave today?" If I raised the shade on my window, written on the window was: "How's Dave today?" That greeting found its way into my coffee cup, beneath my coffee cup, on slides within programs I taught, and virtually anything I picked up either camouflaged the greeting beneath it or contained it thereon.

To the best of my ability I cautioned Paul that "payback can be hell." This did not deter his mission.

Payback #1:
Paul received a message on his desk: "Call Mrs. Smith, Aetna Claims Dept." and a phone number. She was, of course, a friend of mine.

"Hello, this is Paul. I have a message to call you. I don't have insurance with you so I'm baffled why you'd want to speak to me."

She: "Do you have a teenaged son named Tim?"

Trembling: "Yesssss."

She: "Please stay on the line, Paul. I'll have to retrieve the file." With that she sat patiently and timed exactly ten minutes before picking up the telephone again.

She: "I'm terribly sorry, but we've sent that file to our legal department and you'll have to call them," and she gave him the number. (Hint: another friend.)

Paul: "Well, goodness, can't you tell me what this is all about?"

She: "No, sir. I'm sorry. I'm not allowed to discuss it with you. Please call the legal department."

The 'legal department' answered with only the phone number.

Paul: "This is Paul and I'm to understand there is a problem."

She: "Yes, Paul. Please stand by while I retrieve the file. Perhaps we can resolve this."

She sat also patiently for ten minutes before taking up the phone.

She: "Yes, Paul. We have need of only one piece of information to close this file."

Paul: "Yes???"

She: "How's Paul today?"

Now you'd think any rational man would conclude that payback was not only hell, it was time-consuming and admirably original. Nope. "How's Dave Today?" was written on my coffee cup.

Payback #2:
Paul lived about 35 miles from work. He had to leave before 7 a.m. to arrive on time. That is to say: No Post Office was open. On Friday, to arrive on Monday, I sent a <u>Registered, Addressee Only</u> letter to Paul, one for which he had to sign. Naturally he couldn't before work and didn't get home in time afterwards. When I mailed it at the Post Office in the City Center Square building, I dreamed up a P.O. Box number and zip code. Frankly, I thought 64196 was an area of Kansas City and not exclusively City Center Square itself.

Monday morning Paul received a frantic call from home: "There is this registered letter. They won't give it to me. You have to sign for it." Naturally Paul inquired about the return address and learned the return P.O. Box and zip code.

Paul left the office and went to City Center Square. Learning that the zip code was that building and that building only, he inspected the list of occupants in the building. Paul returned quite frustrated, called home and said, "It's the IRS. I think we're getting audited." Could I have scripted this better?

On Saturday morning, having waited all week for this moment of revelation, Paul entered the Post Office as its first customer. He signed for the letter, ripped it open to find a single white card. On it: "How's Paul today?"

Beyond that, Paul was seriously concerned that I smoked cigarettes. There were no restrictions to smoking within the building back then, so I did so comfortably at my desk. Paul and I were separated only by a partition one could stand and peer over. This good-hearted friend was repeatedly encouraging me to 'not smoke': "I care about you. It is not good for you."

The day of the Great American Smoke-Out, I arrived at work to find my entire wall space filled with Smoke-Out posters Scotch-taped on every possible surface. I said, "Paul, you've gone too far. Now I have to take all of these down."

On the way home from work I stopped by the hardware store and bought 15 feet of half-inch tubing. Arriving at work before Paul (who didn't?), I taped one end beneath his desk, ran it under the petition and within my grasp at my desk.

Seeing the manager, I called him over. "You know, both you and Paul have been concerned because I smoke. I'm thinking if I had a better oxygen supply, I might feel better and not be as tempted."

Glenn is grinning. He knows something's up. "And…?"

"Well, watch this." I took a big drag, pulled up the tubing and exhaled all the smoke into it with good pressure.

"Where did that go?"

"Under Paul's desk."

Within the hour Paul was leaning over the partition: "Did you change brands of cigarettes? Man, it's strong in here today!" Some time later he remarked, "There's so much smoke in this room that it's coming out from under my desk."

I was returning from teaching a class when Tom intercepted me: "Paul took your cigarette lighter off of your desk."

I hunted, I fumed, I tossed papers: "Where the heck is that lighter?" Paul suggested that maybe I couldn't smoke now. "No, I'll just walk up to the drugstore and buy another one." I did.

When I returned, Tom asked: "Did you get a lighter?"

"Why, yes I did, Tom. And also I found something I haven't had in a long, long time. A CIGAR."

Few things make me more sick that a cigar. This was a mission of sacrifice and payback. I puffed that cigar and blew it in the tube until I was ready to visit the porcelain goddess. Paul visited the maintenance folks and borrowed a fan for his desk.

Finally Tom couldn't contain the mystery. I saw him stop Paul and could see he was ratting me out by Paul's stunned expression, the word *WHAT!* easy to interpret, and his charge back to his desk. Simple. I just pulled the tube, disconnected it, rolled it up and stuck it in a drawer.

We all stood there and watched Paul on his knees, then his stomach, searching the underside of his desk for 'some tube.' I had to shake my head. "Paul, you have to be one of the most paranoid men I've ever known."

In time I'd Scotch-taped his phone button. You could pick it up to answer, but it kept ringing. Another time I gift-wrapped his telephone. That package was ringing! He tore it apart, finally had access to the phone and the son-of-a-gun quit ringing. I once wrapped his entire desk in duct tape. Another tactic was to move the partition two inches per day toward Paul until he was almost relocated in another aircraft's section.

When Paul left TWA to join UPS, I'd really lost a friend at work. However, I did advise every UPS pilot I met, for years after: "When Paul asks in class if there are any questions, you have one: How's Paul today?"

(Incidentally, this photo is called an "Uh-Oh.")

THE COCKPIT

O n one flight the personality conflict between the captain and copilot was tactile. The captain snarled, "You have to be the most inept, unskilled, and worst copilot on this airline."

The first officer replied: "No, sir. That would be just too much of a scheduling coincidence, wouldn't it?"

===

Renaissance pilot: An aviator possessed of myriad interests and exotic experiences, who, with each passing day is able to recall with greater clarity things that never happened.

===

There was the copilot who made a particularly bad landing and mumbled, "That was the worst landing I've ever made."

The captain replied, "Oh? I wasn't sure you'd ever landed before."

===

A particularly difficult airplane to land is the Boeing 727. After a bad, *bad* landing, the copilot said, "The 727 sure lands funny, doesn't it?"

The Captain snarled, "It wasn't meant to."

===

The Boeing 727 was known as "Miss Piggy" for the absence of performance. One did not attend Recurrent Training, they were "Re-Pigged." One adage was, "If you have 5000 hours in a 727, 4500 of them are in climb." And, "It's a safe airplane. It goes up like a safe and comes down like a safe." Being a "Pig Pilot" or "Flying the Pig" always identified one's assigned equipment.

The Boeing 737 was known as a FLUFF. "Fat Little Ugly (Fellow)" or something more carnal in conclusion. Then there was the military's huge B-52 bombers: BUFF: Big Ugly Fat (Fellow). It was also known as...an Aluminum Cloud.

━━━━

After the abortive 'demonstration' of the Airbus 320 at the Paris Airshow, where it mushed into the trees, the riddle was, "What is the difference between an Airbus and a chain saw?" Answer: "About 300 trees a minute."

━━━━

Heard in a Lufthansa cockpit: "How does an Airbus-340 climb?"

Answer: "By the bend of the earth."

━━━━

Heard over the PA during a landing roll: "Whoa, big fellow. WHOA!"

━━━━

When I checked out as a copilot on the DC-9, we were enroute to Indianapolis at night. All the little cities and town glistened in little clusters below us amid the darkness.

The captain asked: "Has anyone pointed out these little cities to you before?"

In the old days captains could name every one of them, coast to coast. I replied, "No, sir."

"Well, there is one to the left, and another over there, and here's one up ahead of us, and about six down south…" (and so on).

I was flying a trip from Dallas to Honolulu and as we passed Los Angeles I made the obligatory announcement: "We're crossing the California coastline. That's L.A. on the left and we'll be in Honolulu in about four hours."

Half an hour later, a flight attendant came to the cockpit choked in laughter: "A lady in coach wants to know what big lake we're flying over?"

"Tell her it's Lake Pacificia."

—Capt. George Shanks (American-Retired).

One of the great sights crossing Arizona is Meteor Crater, an impact from 50,000 years ago and in which you could submerge many football fields. A flight attendant came to the cockpit to deliver coffee and the DC-10 offered a magnificent view. Noting the 'hole,' she asked the Captain about it. He explained it was Meteor Crater. She stared a moment and commented, "Wow, it just missed that parking lot, didn't it?"

—Capt. George Shanks (American-Retired).

One of our first female Captains was Shelly, a former U.S. Air Force aviator, a command pilot on the C-141 and a fine lady. A father and small child came to the cockpit and Shelly greeted them with her usual gracious hospitality. As they left she overheard the child say, "Dad, the captain is a flight attendant!"

═══

On most aircraft requiring flight engineers, he would set 'climb power.' The captain would handle the throttles for takeoff, the first officer would finely tune them, and at some point the captain would call, "Climb Power" (the F/E's job).

One airline installed a video camera in the cockpit by which the passengers could enjoy the cockpit environment on takeoff or landing, whichever the Captain permitted them to observe on the video screen.

The crew conspired for the flight engineer to have a gorilla's 'arm,' a sleeve easily slipped on his hand, up to his elbow. When climb power was called for, this hairy arm was visible reaching to do so.

Thereafter, the passengers could see the captain handing the 'animal' a banana.

═══

One airline's first officer got so tongue-tied on a transmission that every effort got more confused as he repeated the effort.

Anonymous transmission: "Hire the handicapped!"

═══

Within the system we had a Jewish copilot who was very, very sensitive to any comment or attitude he considered anti-Semitic. We had one grizzly old captain who delighted in baiting him. After the captain flew the first leg, he'd ask, "Di'yew wanna fly?" which sounded awfully like "Jew wanna fly?"

He thought he was offended, but it just wasn't enunciated well enough to claim insult.

―――――

We had one domestic captain who was particularly nasty to flight attendants, on the plane, in the crew van, even at the hotel. He never had anything nice to say, and injected himself unkindly responding to anything one of the ladies did say. As the month ended and I never had to fly with him again, I found his flight bag, carried it to ticketing desk and said, "I'm deadheading over to London. Would you check my flight bag to Heathrow so it's there when I fly the airplane back?"

I don't know how long his flight bag sat in London before he recovered it, nor did I care. Those were the days before tight security.

―――――

The crew had been on duty for about fourteen hours and were very tired. Their uniforms were wrinkled and dirty, and they looked like five o'clock shadow razor advertisements. One very obviously gay male flight attendant came to the cockpit and just oozed the comment, "You guys look tired."

"Yeah, we've been on duty a long time," answered the flight engineer.

"What you guys need is a shot and a beer," he gushed.

The captain swirled around, enraged: "Just get the H--- out of here. I don't go for that." The captain was a genuinely gentle fellow, easy to get along with, never harsh or cruel in comment, and his response had the other two baffled. Then he mumbled, "Did you hear that homosexual sumbitch tell us we needed a shot in the rear?"

The copilot and flight engineer were nearly hysterical with laughter and the Captain learned he may have a bit of hearing damage from years in aviation.

====

This is too cute to even camouflage the name: Wayne Boyd. If one thinks our homes weren't saturated with aviation and everyone's mind so attuned, Wayne called a friend of his. The young daughter asked who was calling: "Wayne Boyd." When Dad answered the phone, he was roaring with laughter. His daughter told him, "Wing Boeing is calling."

====

In Charlotte, North Carolina one of the ramp agents was a tall, lovely, African-American lady named Virginia. She is too classy and kind to ever suspect subterfuge. She plugged in her headset at the forward receptacle to clear us for pushback. She said, "Ground to cockpit, do you read?"

"No."

"Ground to cockpit, do you read me now?

"No."

"Wait a minute and I'll replug in the headset. Do you hear me now?"

"NO, I don't."

"But you're answering me!"

"Yes, I am anticipating what you're asking me and attempting to help, but I can't hear you."

"Wait a minute and I'll get another headset."

She left, walked to the ramp office and returned with another headset.

"Can you hear me now?"

"Just barely, Virginia. You're gonna have to really scream."

I'm sure pilots at the next five adjoining gates heard Virginia giving us clearance to pressurize, release the brakes and push back. Sweet lady. I was never able to pull that again with her.

My late, best friend Jim Mandigo had just checked out on the 707. Jim was so hyper he made me look like a walking Xanax. All the passengers wanted to know the score of the World Series. The captain, a big gentle, fun-loving bear of a man, told Jim that he could make the announcement. Jim got the PA handset and was Jim-hyper ready, while the Captain tuned in the ADF radio to a broadcast frequency.

"Get ready, Jim, they are about to give the score."

Jim is wired to ready, breath already taken, a professional broadcast forthcoming.

"Tell them it is 3-to-1 in the top of the first inning."

Jim was spring-loaded and did that. It took the flight attendant about five seconds to knock on the door to state the passengers thought the pilot must be nuts or never played baseball.

===

We had one captain who was the nicest possible guy, but who could not relinquish control of the airplane. When it was the copilot's leg (or segment) , unexpected things would happen. Without warning the captain might lower the gear in his belief you were too high or extend more flaps. The result was a rather surprising control change or attitude pitch adjustment that one didn't expect. He was always nice, mumbling, "I thought you were too high and wanted to help." So in the ramp office someone asked me what it is like to fly with John.

"Well, you'll find that he will fly a leg, then WE get to fly a leg."

===

The Boeing 707 was a glorious bird, the Queen of the Airways in her day. It had a big three- or four-inch circular Boeing 707 nameplate and logo right in the middle of the control yoke that you could pull out. Pull it off they did. Back in those days we were all young and feisty and *decorated* the cockpit. We had no female crewmembers. Pilots would put in lovely pinup pictures, comments about the Chief Pilot or the best of cartoons inserted inside that control yoke Boeing logo plate. We'd sit down, pull it off, examine the art left for us and comment on its selection.

This got the FAA's attention. An inspector wrote us up, "I noted that TWA pilots are the only ones whose preflight inspection in the cockpit includes examining the safety wiring of the control yoke behind a Boeing identity plate."

Hey, we were thorough!

We don't have flight engineers anymore. That position had a unique role in airline aviation and on the plane: They occupied the only seat that faced sideways and did not flush.

Everyone admires another who has deep religious conviction. I doubt that pompousness and righteousness are the tenets of many Western religions we know. At another airline one captain always cautioned his first officers to have their seat forward, the control yoke within easy reach and feet ready to command the rudder pedals: "Because if Rapture comes, you might find yourself alone up here."

Surely it was within the authority of the captain to dictate to the Lord which of the two deserved to be Raptured. We'll never know if the captain ultimately finds himself alone in the cockpit.

One of the best jobs on the airlines in the 1950s and 1960s was to be a reserve pilot. Like the extra-board on the railroads, the reserve pilot was subject to call when needed for an unexpected opening. The contract back then stated he need be *only* "reasonably available." The reserve pilot had a pay guarantee and not a bad income for rarely working. We had some who were 'reasonably *unavailable*' for months. One senior flight engineer had grieved the schedulers and they tired of his absence to take a call. They finally called his home at four a.m. His wife answered.

"This is TWA scheduling calling Flight Engineer Martin."

She: "I'm sorry, he's not here. He's at the barber shop."

I always thought that should you should answer the phone when Scheduling called at that time of morning, you should say, "Just a minute." In a loud whisper to your wife, "It's your husband's employer calling for him."

═══

It's not that way anymore. Reserves have two-hour and six-hour call-out assignments, designated telephone check-in times and far more restrictions. Nonetheless, we see humor. In the 'old days' all the schedulers knew their pilots, knew who to ask for a favor and knew who would meet an emergency with enthusiasm. Then we went to computers. Impersonal.

At San Diego, a copilot arrived for the flight, feeling ill, but hoping he could take the trip. He finally yielded to the intense pain and apologized for taking himself off the trip at the last minute. Our computerized, electronic genius in Scheduling decided to delay a Los Angeles flight by two hours, seize the first officer from that flight, and fly him to San Diego to continue the crew-crippled trip. In turn, they would call out the reserve pilot to replace the usurped pilot in Los Angeles. As the San Diego-bound pilot was flying southbound, the reserve pilot—yes, you guessed it, a resident of San Diego—was flying northbound to Los

Angeles to replace him. In many ways the Y2K bug would have been a blessing.

———

My first trip to Las Vegas, how exciting. As the Boeing 707 crested the mountains in descent about midnight, a billion candlepower radiated out of the darkness of the desert. One multi-colored glow of lights that was awesome. I was awed, in fact.

"Gee," I said, "Does it always look like that?"

"Nope," said the Captain. "Come in here about noon and you can't see any lights at all."

———

I had one unexpected, unprecedented aircraft damage event. We landed at Norfolk. We were parked off the jetway. We waited for the ramp signalman. He arrived in a blue Chevrolet, stopped it, leaped from it and began the approach-me signals. I was focused on him. After I parked the brakes, the plane was shocked sideways by impact.

"Wow," I remarked, "someone is pretty rough with that baggage belt loader."

The ground phone was plugged in now: "Captain, you've just been hit by a car. You'd better come look."

The lad had leaped from the Chevrolet and it slipped into reverse gear by itself. The car in reverse circled our left wing without incident, circled the tail without impact, around the right wing without crisis and veered into the aircraft at the forward baggage compartment. The airplane's conical shape allowed the car to pull itself midway beneath the plane, shattering the rear windshield and crushing the top of the car.

Irony: The boy had no security ID to be on the airport property and his driver's license had been suspended the week before.

—————

Now retired, I ride in the back of the plane. That used to be agony, particularly in uniform. Once the passengers knew you were a pilot, you had to hear about every bad flight, lost baggage, rude flight attendant, delay or cancellation. Now I travel conducting radar seminars and typically in a sports suit. Nonetheless, other passengers want to talk and I don't. There are two tactics, suggested to me by the creative Rod Machado, that I share with you to maintain your isolation and be left alone.

If your seatmate asks you what you do for a living, you reply: "I collect funds for religious cults." (You are guaranteed to be left alone.)

If you get to speak first, you stretch your arms and announce, "There is no better day than your first day out of prison." (You are guaranteed to be left alone.)

—————

From my friend retired Captain George Shanks, American Airlines:

Once on the 727 and heading west toward a dissipating thunderstorm, the cloud shape looked like the east end of a westbound whale.

The F/O commented, "Look at that cloud. It looks like a whale's tail."

George couldn't resist. "Aw, it's just a fluke."

———

No airport was constructed with the agony of Denver's mega-million-dollar facility: DIA. The jokes were plentiful: DIA...Debacle In Automation, Dare I Ask?, Dumb Idea Anyway, Denver's Imaginary Airport, Dysfunction Imitating Art and Dazzling Inaccessible Airport. The consummate and disabling problem was the 4000-plus baggage carts that were computerized to route and deliver bags from the plane. In attempting to discover the problem, they mounted a video camera on one cart and began its route. They lost it. Since we were still landing at Stapleton, the old airport, I could never resist a cabin announcement passing the soon-to-open DIA:

"Ladies and Gentlemen. If you look to the right you'll see Denver's new airport...so new...it doesn't even look USED yet, does it?"

Or: "This is the Captain and off to your left is Denver's new airport. If we are all very, very quiet, you can hear 4000 little baggage carts all chanting: I think I can...I think I can."

———

Cabin announcements could be fun: "Off to the left, ladies and gentlemen, is Omaha...or maybe that's Tulsa. But we're right on schedule."

———

As our country became aware of a growing drug problem, it wasn't long before all transportation personnel were random drug tested. It's been really nonsense.

Marijuana is stored in fatty tissue and may be detected up to 30 days. That's about the only value. Cocaine, in example, is metabolized and gone in three days. So if one were a user, he should bid four-day trips since we knew we were never tested until our return to the domicile. Why not before the trip? Well, shucks, folks, you'd have to have reserves available if someone didn't pass and that's expensive. Nonetheless, we all had to submit to that first drug test. When I arrived at the doctor's office, Captain Gary was waiting, too. The nurse-receptionist was cool and really rather cruel in her harsh greeting, a not-nice lady.

I sat beside Gary and began my litany: "You know, Gary, without any professional help whatever, I gave up sniffing coke." (The nurse's head snapped to attentiveness; Gary ducked behind his paper, grinning.) "I don't know how they do it. That carbonation really irritated my nasal passages. You have to let that can sit there an hour or two before you try to breathe it. I'm thinking about sniffing Diet 7-Up. Maybe less sugar or carbonation can let me enjoy the experience."

The nurse snapped, "I'll bet you think you're funny, don't you?"

I replied, "Yes, ma'am. I truly am. You're just the only one who can't recognize it."

A friend was based in LAX and was so junior that he was F/E on a 707 all-night freighter. (Is all-night freighter redundant?) He was on a layover at the Boston Hilton. He and the other two pilots were standing out front in uniform at about 10 p.m. waiting on a limo. Some self-important jerk drove up in a new Cadillac and pitched the keys to John, directing him, "Here, park this." John looked at the keys, thought a minute, and said to his crew, "Okay guys, let's go." They left the Caddy in the parking lot at the freight terminal.

—Retired Captain Tom Travis–American Airlines

Ah, the good old days of long layovers. A friend once told me that the way you could tell a good hotel was when you could only get one of their towels in your suitcase.

—Retired Captain Tom Travis–American Airlines

Taxiing in St. Louis, some pilot observed the Southwest 737 painted like Shamu, the black and white whale at Sea World. We all howled to hear him transmit, "Hey, there's an airplane out here with a whale shoved up its butt."

Back in the Braniff Airlines days, their airplanes were painted in many vivid colors. One was brown, and the paint became weathered, dull and ugly. On ground control frequency some pilot asked, "Good Lord, Braniff. *What* did you fly through?"

They also had one painted pumpkin-orange. The Braniff pilots themselves had fun with that one: "Tower, the Great Pumpkin is ready to leave the patch."

A Captain might know procedures, but not protocol on another airline, especially a foreign carrier. Long ago , the USA Captain was jump-seating on Air _____ , based in a country where the Captain was not only God, but empowered as such. Being familiar with the Boeing 727 he watched their procedures, virtually identical to his own airline's. At cruise the foreign-carrier Captain asked, "Do you do anything different than we do?"

"Well, yes. After raising the gear, we lower the gear level to the neutral position to cut off the hydraulic flow to the gear system."

The host Captain backhanded his First Officer, who immediately put the gear level in the middle-neutral position and turned crimson with the error (and the blow, no doubt).

"We do the same," El Capitáno announced.

Of course the American pilot felt terrible to see such consequences from an innocent observation.

The young Flight Engineer was reporting to the Chief Pilot who asked his name. "John, sir."

"Until you're a Captain or a friend, young man, I'll address you by your last name. What is it?"

"Darling, sir."

"Okay, John. I have a couple things to discuss with you."

Yes, there was an occasional one-night romance, but in the distant past. One copilot met, wined and dined a flight attendant and affection was generated. Enhancing the *conversation* in her room, she demanded "protection" before the discussion continued. He grabbed sufficient clothing to dash downstairs to the drug store. Returning to the elevators he realized he'd forgotten what room she was in, didn't know her last name, nor even by what flight she arrived to check the crew registry. One dejected and the other apparently rejected, I suppose.

—Contributed Anonymously

One of my dearest friends of decades and a well-known personality had a NYC layover as a young copilot. It was on this trip that he ventured to enchant a new, young flight attendant.

"Would you like to go to dinner and see a Broadway show?"

She was more excited than Bill Clinton reading the singles ads!

After the show she was gushing her appreciation, praising his generosity and cultured personality. He had to top it.

"Would you like to have a drink at Sardi's?"

"Oh magawd! A drink at Sardi's?! I'd love it."

He'd never been to Sardi's in his life. They entered one of the waiting cabs and he said; "Sardi's, please."

"WHAT?" the cab driver answered with some alarm.

"*Take us* to Sardi's. What could be simpler?"

"Okay."

The cab driver made a U-Turn in the street, stopped and announced, "Here's Sardi's."

It was across the street. I guess you had to have been there before to know that.

I had to ask, "What'd you do?"

"I gave him ten bucks and told her, 'Nothing but the best for you, babe'."

———

The most common expression heard in the cockpit used to be, "Was that for us?"

Now with the computerized flight management systems, it's, "What's it doing now? Where is it taking us?"

———

Prior to the 1960s the Captain was unassailable, the commander, a *bona fide* SkyGod who happily challenged the Chief Pilot. One airline had a couple of incidents where drinking was alleged and by which an altercation occurred on a layover. Not only did that company issue a bulletin, but made every pilot sign an acknowledgement that forbade drinking any amount, any beverage of alcohol, on any layover, regardless of the down time.

Rumor had it that they had hired Pinkerton's Detective Agency to follow crews and observe layover conduct.

A friend of mine was on a long layover with a senior captain, and they stopped in for a beer before dinner. The captain struck up a conversation with the chap to his right,

"What do you do for a living?"

"I'm a detective."

"Who do you work for?"

"Pinkerton's."

"Doing what?"

"I'm assigned to follow _____ Airlines crews to catch any drinking on layovers."

The Captain said calmly, "Well, you ain't doing a very G–d— good job of it." The copilot split and cannot report any more of the conversation.

Then in the 80s and 90s we had a couple of incidents with irresponsible and immature pilots that took the humor out of the scenario.

Retired Captain George Shanks liked to recall a new-hire Flight Engineer who ultimately became V.P. of Flight Operations. Not a timid man. One first officer was consummately inconsiderate. He'd order coffee, never finish it and hand it to the Flight Engineer on takeoff. "Here, do something with this."

Most F/Es tried to hold on to it and had coffee stains on their shirts and clothes. Not this chap! "Sure," and then he'd pour the coffee in the F/O's flight bag. It seems the F/O finally got the message and ceased making that abusive demand.

Another memorable captain in the Shanks career believed airplanes were to be flown fast and taxied the same way. In El Paso, Runway 8 was very close to the gate. The Captain cranked it up, taxied out like a race car, took off and told the F/E, "Report out of the gate at :30 and off at :31."

Soon the F/E stated, "Captain, Dispatch is questioning your out-and-off times."

"Tell them :30 and :31. Delay account of ground traffic."

From *Australian Aviation* magazine:

After a lousy landing by the first officer, the Captain picked up the P.A. microphone and stated, "Ladies and gentlemen, we apologize for that rough landing provided today by our copilot."

Several months later, the two were together again and the Captain assaulted the earth with an arrival that left dents in the cement. The first officer grabbed the P.A. microphone and said, "Ladies and gentlemen, we hasten to apologize for that rough landing provided today by the Captain."

Angrily: "Why did you do that!"

The copilot replied with a grin, "Because you did it to me!"

"Yeah," said the captain, "but I never keyed the microphone."

In the cockpit we listened to the appropriate air traffic control frequency, but we also monitored the airplane interphone system for any calls from the flight attendants. In an emergency they were to pick up the microphone and begin talking, knowing that we were on the system.

One day we had an abrupt and demanding controller (a bad hair day) who got rude in his clearances and responses to virtually anything. He handed us off to another frequency.

I replied, "Roger, contact Center on 135.6," and flipping my microphone over to interphone, I added, "And why don't you go screw yourself, you arrogant bastard."

If I hadn't calmed the captain and his impending stroke, I might have gained a seniority number that day.

===

Reported at San Jose:

A DC-10 Heavy aircraft made a fast approach, touching down well beyond the landing zone.

Tower: "_____ 751-Heavy turn right at the end if able. If not, take the Guadalupe exit off Highway 101 back to the airport."

===

After spending several million dollars to permit Senator John Glenn to both revisit space and determine the effects on the elderly, the adventure was a scientific success: "It was verified that dental adhesive works in zero gravity."

===

One retired pilot told me, "Yes, there are days I miss the airline life. We have a routine at my house. I set the alarm for 4 a.m., get up, get dressed and pack a bag. My wife places a chair in our small, cramped pantry, sets a cold breakfast on my lap and closes the door. I eat that with minimal light. At the same time she runs the vacuum cleaner outside the door. Ya know, by the time I'm done, I just don't miss it anymore."

===

PILOT RULES:

The CAPTAIN makes the rules.

The rules are subject to change without prior notification.

NO copilot can possibly know, or is permitted to know, all of the rules.

IF the CAPTAIN suspects the copilot knows the rules, they must be changed in part (preferably 'in total').

The CAPTAIN is never wrong.

IF the CAPTAIN is wrong, it is due to a misunderstanding conveyed to him by the copilot.

The copilot must apologize, tear his clothing in grief and pour ashes upon his head.

The CAPTAIN may change his mind at any time.

The copilot may not change his mind about any topic without permission of the CAPTAIN. (Permission in writing is standard policy).

The CAPTAIN may be angry, upset, rude or abusive at any time with or without due cause.

The copilot must remain calm, unless directed to be angry or upset by the CAPTAIN ('rude and abusive' is not permissible even by written permission).

The CAPTAIN is ready when he is ready.

The copilot must be ready at all times, and in fact, clairvoyant as to the CAPTAIN's state of readiness.

No copilot may document the rules, imply that he knows them or convey the rules to other copilots. This places an undue burden on the CAPTAIN who must then recreate new rules without sufficient time.

When It Rains…Everyone Knows:
It seems that when an airline has a problem (and all do) two or three others occur for maximum publicity and embarrassment. The much-respected Delta airlines had a flight land at the wrong airport one night (two close-by and similar airports made it possible by making the approach visually, without electronic aid). So the pilots created the advertising assertion:

DELTA….meaning "Don't Ever Land There Again."
(Also: "A real man lands anywhere he wants to.")

With an evacuation near that time, it was expanded:
DELTA….Your kids will love our big yellow slides.
(With apologies to Delta, my own choice of airlines in my business travels.)

One airline had the top of the fuselage leave the airplane due to metal fatigue, open skies in First Class. We thought an appropriate advertising theme was:
"Three classes of service: First Class, Coach and Patio."
OR: "Get your tan before you land."

SECURITY

The beginning of security screening seemed undisciplined. It seemed they especially liked to harass the flight crews. With the control yoke in our hands, AND a crash ax in the cockpit, nonetheless, we were screened, circled with the wand, even hand-searched to assure we were not a hazard to the flight.

We sure applauded Capt. Bob Kupferberg, our ALPA Chairman. In his disgust, Bob showed up at the airport in the wee hours (minimal audience), took off his pants and coat, and walked through screening in his shorts. Bravo, Bobby!

On one occasion the young man told me, "Your wings are setting off the alarm. Take them off." I replied, "Wouldn't it be simpler for me to take off my COAT and send it through the X-ray?" He reluctantly agreed.

At one of the smaller California airports, I continued to set off the alarm. Every pocket was emptied, my shoes were off, and I had the wand and hand search. In my haste to leave home, I had unfortunately put on a belt with some elements of silver inlay. "Take off your belt." After a half-dozen trips through the machine, in stocking feet, hand-searched and given the wand, I'd had it. "*If* it is my belt, then you have determined that. I will not get undressed for you. I will not take off any more clothing, even a belt. You can notify the station manager that the flight is delayed or cancelled. I don't care." I grabbed all my clothing, shoes, bags and retreated to a seat to get dressed again. The Security Supervisor came over to plead with me. Still miffed, I said, "NO. I haven't even mentioned that I have a crash ax in the cockpit, but you've pushed me too far." After a puzzled pause, he said, "Okay, Captain, just go around the machine and to your flight." (I could not resist the comment that "with enough anger on my part, you're willing to bypass your issue in total, right?")

None of this equals my effort to smuggle a 'simulated weapon' on the plane. After speaking in the FAA Building at Sun 'n Fun, friends and I gathered to have some hot dogs at the picnic tables. A deaf-mute came by, handing out his cards to solicit money. Attached to the card was a small keychain, with a copper-tone Army .45 pistol, less than *three-quarters of an inch* in length.

I gave him a couple dollars, pocketed the gift in my sport coat pocket and forgot it. Going through St. Louis, I dashed up to check my mail, then attempted to go through security. When I emptied my pockets, there was 'a replica of a weapon.' The elderly security screener snatched it up, grabbed my arm and told me I would be escorted to the supervisor. First I said, "Take your hands off of me. Give me back my TWA ID card."

I was escorted to an office. The female in charge had the 'weapon' pinched between her forefinger and thumb, holding it up to inspect it. I said, "Lethal looking, isn't it?" She snarled at me, "Do you think this is funny?" I replied, "Yes, ma'am. I think it's hysterical."

She advised me that it was a seized item and if I wanted it back I should leave my name, address and employee ID number. "Perhaps the police will give it back to you." I was sympathetic that "this is so important to you that I want you to have it."

The next day I called my pal Lou Voog in TWA's Legal Department and relayed the story. She: "I have to get that. What a kick it will be to toss it on the table next week when I meet with FAA Security." Guess what? It had disappeared. It could not be located. We also learned that screeners (at that time) got a $100 bonus for seizure of weapons. My toy met the description: Replica of a weapon.

In Korea you were required to take off your shoes, but not expose your computer. They did object to my having four extra Triple-A batteries in my carry-on luggage. I had to forfeit them. In France, I spoke too soon: "Good morning!" Ah, an American! I was all but strip-searched.

"I think we can buff that out."

PERSONALITIES

Naturally we had many prominent personalities travel on TWA, and one Pope called us Traveling With Angels. We had many Senators and Sandra Day O'Connor, with whom I spoke briefly. Baseball legends George Brett and Lou Brock were totally enjoyable gentlemen. Ray Charles was as charming as you might image him to be. In Vegas, I visited briefly with Liberace on the jetway and at length with kind, humble boxing great Joe Lewis at Caesars. Buddy Hackett, despite his nightclub act, was one of the kindest, most friendly persons I met. General Matt Ridgway (who replaced General MacArthur) was a longtime friend and I attended his 85th birthday party. Robert Young (Dr. Welby) was also a longtime friend, and we visited by phone about twice a month. Despite Bob's paternal TV personality, Bob could outswear nine sailors when he was miffed over some matter of ethics.

In the 1970s I met often with Evel Knievel, arranging pilots for him. Once we waited for him until 10 p.m. He had to cancel. He arrived in a beat-up Chevrolet that he borrowed from a janitor, came to the airport because we weren't available by phone and gave each of the linemen $50 checks for the inconvenience he'd caused. A generous man!

I had a delightful three-hour lunch with Werner von Braun, and a lengthy conversation in flight with Howard Cosell. Mr. Cosell was a wonderful conversationalist. This was during the raging "hate Howard Cosell" campaign in the football arenas. He confessed how much it hurt him to be so disliked. "I never received a piece of hate mail until I defended Muhammad Ali in his refusal to be drafted. You cannot strip a man of his title with an indictment, only a conviction. I spoke up for him and 75% of my mail thereafter was hate mail. He was denied due process of law."

In First Class I was seated with a big man, jeans and cowboy boots. On his finger was a "Miller's All Stars" ring. I've never been a football fan, so did not recognize him: Ben Davidson, former (mean!) linebacker for the Oakland Raiders. I asked him, "Do you miss football?" He said, "I sure don't miss getting hurt!"

In 1976 I was on the ramp at K.C. Downtown Airport when a limo arrived with Ronald Reagan in it. He'd been defeated for the nomination by Gerry Ford and was going home. We visited as he waited for the rest of his staff. He was a superbly outgoing and friendly man. As they boarded, Nancy looked down at us and waved, with tears in her eyes. I took a picture. When Reagan was elected President I sent the picture to Nancy with a note: "I'll bet things are better now." She replied with a very nice letter (and agreed).

During the Reagan Administration I was invited to speak in Omaha for Nancy Reagan's "Just Say No Campaign," called The White House Conference on a

Drug-Free America. It dealt strictly with illegal drugs. I enjoyed meeting Gayle Sayers, football legend, who confirmed that the movie "Brian's Song" was perfectly accurate. At the Governor's Coffee Party, I saw a gentleman in a tuxedo who I knew I'd met before. We locked eyes at one point; he smiled and waved. I walked over to him: "I know we've met and please forgive me for not remembering your name." It was Mike Connors, TV's "Mannix."

Of all the personalities, perhaps the most timid, shy and self-conscious was Chuck Berry, rock-and-roll Hall of Famer. A nice man. Kiefer Sutherland flew with us to Canada. Peter Fonda was an outgoing chap in first class. Hal Linden and Andy Williams were total gentlemen and nice to meet.

I did not ever match the enjoyment of my pal, Barry Schiff when he was a copilot on Martin 404s. The Duke was to be on board—John Wayne. In those days security was not a focus, so Duke was invited to ride in the cockpit. Barry: "Bigger than life. So genuine that you loved the guy, in his jeans, cowboy boots and western hat." He rode the whole trip visiting with the pilots.

At Fairfax Airport I landed a charter, and saw a plane that I couldn't identify. The pilots told me it was a Fokker F-29 (as I recall) and invited me aboard. Wow! Plush! Even a bedroom in back. They told me it was leased airplane. Behind one chair I saw a cardboard, gilt guitar with "Boston Loves Elvis" on it. "Is this Presley's airplane?" It was. He was performing downtown. We drank some coffee, visited about flying Elvis and they announced:

"He'll be here in 11 minutes. We have to get ready." ("11 minutes?" "Yes, this is timed to the minute.") I walked to the stairs, where two lines of people had gathered to tell Elvis goodbye. As I walked down, three limos tore around that field in great haste. Everyone rushed on board except Elvis, who shook hands and thanked everyone in the departure party. When he got me, I said, "Mr. Presley, I'm just an outsider. I'm not supposed to be here." He smiled: "Ah, that's all right. It's good to see you." The right engine was turning on the airplane. As he stepped inside, the left engine began to rotate and the stairs to retract.

When that airplane rotated for takeoff on Runway 36, about a thousand cars arrived at that airport, attempting to catch Elvis before he left. Timed to the minute! That was about 1973. He looked good. I was surprised how he seemed to tower over me, and with shoulders that looked like he could take your head off with one swing.

I was privileged to meet a lot of people. Those that I treasured most, however, were in the field of aviation: Richard Bach, the late Gordon Baxter, Richard Collins, Hal Shevers, John and Martha King, my editors previously mentioned, and Capt. Al Haynes, the master of cockpit management in the Sioux City tragedy. Most of all, my "bestest buddies" Rod Machado and Barry Schiff, two friendships that I treasure.

Tribute to Aleksandr Zuyev

When I spoke at the Washington State Aviation Convention and Trade Show, I met Alex Zuyev. He'd written a book titled *Fulcrum*, and other than that I knew nothing of him.

He spoke that night at the banquet and everyone was awestruck. Alex had defected from the Soviet Union with a M-29 in 1989. We lost him in the unexplained crash of a Yak-52, which did not recover from an accelerated stall in 2001.

Alex had appeared on *60 Minutes*, *Larry King Live* and *Good Morning America*. He brought Valium saturated Brownies to work, inducing sleep among all his Soviet pilot contemporaries. He did engage a guard on his way to seize the plane and disabled the guard (without explanation beyond that). Alex was, however, shot in the right arm.

He flew at Mach .96, 650 miles per hour, at 90 to 100 feet above the ground, both sides attempting to take him out of the air. Captain Zuyev had been a Top Gun fighter pilot for the USSR, guiding his plane to Turkey's border while identical MiGs pursued him.

After his escape he found himself a well-guarded CIA asset and a target of the Soviet KGB. His information unlocked many mysteries, including the shootdown of Korean Airlines Flight 007, and the real story of American POWs taken from Vietnam to the Soviet Union. At one Paris Air Show, he and some journalists approached the Soviet display of a MiG-29, and he was treated with verbal scorn and rejection by his former comrades. That made good TV coverage.

In my time spent with him, I agree with those who labeled him irrepressible, with a great love for this country, and an abundant love of life. He was utterly humble about his achievements, daring escape and masterful skill that made it possible.

In the doomed plane with Alex was Jerry Warren, one of the most famous Cessna 150 pilots. It was Jerry who, in 1998, was tangled upside down in power lines in a Cessna 150, awaiting escape that took four hours to accomplish. Jerry remarked afterwards, "This is really ruining my morning." Jerry also made the *Guinness Book of Records* for the "lowest airplane rescue."

Alex's infectious smile, gentle nature and hearty laughter is gone. He was a hero in my book. I'm glad to have met him and to have spent time with him.

MEMORIES OF DAD AND ELEANOR

As a student at Washington University (St. Louis), Eleanor Roosevelt, FDR's widow, visited and spoke to a small group. My dad suffered in the Depression. He revered President Roosevelt, the only man elected four times to the Presidency (and before we learned a lot about him). Dad was Vice President of a 101,000-member railroad labor union, with bylaws so rigid that it was the only union in which the FBI Director would accept Honorary Membership (before we found out about him too!)

I got to visit with Mrs. Roosevelt on a one-to-one basis and conveyed the great sadness in our home with the death of FDR. She commented, "That's sweet. I have a press conference at 7 p.m. at the Chase Hotel. I'm in room 1037. Please come and we can visit afterwards."

I called Dad. He was elated. "Son, she is history and you've been invited to participate in it." The next morning he was on the phone at 7 a.m. "What did you and Mrs. Roosevelt talk about?" I had to say, "Dad, I had a date with a gorgeous co-ed. I didn't go to the Chase Hotel." Silence…then his receiver hit the cradle in anger or disgust. Well, the flawed perspective of youth has always existed.

THE SPIN (AUTHOR UNKNOWN)

I know that I was told
Nor to err and not to sin
To be gentle and not be bold
But No! I had to spin.

The wing went down
The nose went down
My eyes I tried to cover
As I dropped toward fields of brown

I was determined to be brave
As the rapid rotation became a blur
But I knew this airplane must be saved
This I must do I knew for sure

The spinning now became more rapid
My heart was pounding ever so hard
So do this crazy thing I must be stupid
I know I'll crash in some poultry yard

Now to remember, my instructor said
Relax, be calm, don't be uptight
This was said by instructor Ted
I knew then I would be all right

I thrust forward with opposite rudder
Forward with the elevators, my head hit the top
The rotation stopped with a slight shudder
Then of a sudden my fears came to a stop

Back on the ground and not so tense
I reviewed again what Ted had said a lot
It all sounded easy and made good sense
Would I do it again? Why the hell not!

HERE'S A BREAK FOR YOU !

WHOA, BIG FELLOW! WHOA!

MEMORIES OF MAJOR AIRPORTS

A Pan Am 747 was cleared for takeoff near sunset, ending a bright sunny day, and flying across the Pacific to one of their exotic locations. At the time, many American pilots were flying on contract for JAL (Japanese Airlines), and I suspect one of them made the culminating comments in this exchange:

Departure: "Pan Am, you have a JAL 747, 2 o'clock and high."

Pan Am: "Okay, we're looking. We don't see him."

(Later) Pan Am: "Departure, we're still looking. Where's JAL now?"

Departure: "Still 1 or 2 o'clock and high."

Pan Am: "No, we can't see him."

The JAL Captain came on the frequency in a heavily Japanese accented voice: "Perhaps that's because we come at you with the sun at our backs."

Howling laughter in all cockpits.

Then JAL added: "Yankee dog never learn."

===

In Chicago there was a controller with a sense of humor that was incomparable. He loved his job and the exchanges with pilots. Bless those foreign carriers. I can't master two languages and they must, English being the international aviation language.

Air Mexicana: "Chica'go Control, Air Mexi'cana climb to one-five thou-san'."

Departure (heavy Spanish accent): "Por favor, Air Mexi'cana, clim' to one-five thou-san', Señor."

Delta: "Departure, Delta 305, climbing to fifteen."

Control: "Shucky durn, Delta, y'all climb on up to fifteen, bubba."

Air Mexicana: "Chica'go, you no make fun of me!"

Control: "Pardon', Mexi'cana, I no make fun of *you*. I make fun *of Delta*."

===

Mexicana at JFK:

It is especially frustrating for all concerned when two pilots, both of whom fly well, but 'no hablo Inglise' in duet. Mexicana had missed at least two turn-offs in the taxi to the runway.

Ground: "Air Mexicana, you've done it again. You missed Golf. Now turn left on Hotel."

Mexicana: "Ro'er." (sounds like "Roy-yer")

Ground: "Now you've passed Hotel, Air Mexicana. Turn left on Juliette."

Mexicana: "Ro'er."

I suspect the intra-cockpit thinking was, "Juliette or Huliette? That's an H?" At any rate, they passed Juliette and the ground controller blew!

Ground: "Okay, that's IT, Air Mexicana. You turn left on the next taxiway and stop that airplane. *Do not call me. I'll call you.* You've caused too much confusion. Turn, stop, wait and I'll call you when I have time to work with you."

On that airport, *some* amused and creative pilot transmitted, "Okay, Gringo Yankee Dog!"

Next came Air Mexicana: "Was not us! Was not us!"

＝＝＝＝

There was an old story, perhaps a joke or even actual history, of the airline captain in the 1960s who was flying his first trip into Munich, Germany. Once on the ground he became hopelessly lost, missing turns, finally asking for what became known as 'progressive taxi' (i.e., 'tell me what to do').

Ground with disdain: "Haven't you been to Munich before?"

Captain: "Yes…in 1944, but we didn't land."

＝＝＝＝

Several years ago we had a considerate Flight Engineer conducting the aircraft preflight walkaround. It was a hot day and a poodle was in a kennel in the forward compartment. He felt such empathy that he extracted the dog to hold and nurture it a few minutes. We next saw him chasing a passenger's poodle across the ramp. But that story is reminiscent of an event in the prop-driven Constellation days and in Phoenix.

The were transporting a big dog of the apparently German Shepherd breed. It was a scorching day and that poor animal was trapped in a cage. The ramp agent felt such pity for the dog that he pulled him from the kennel, looped his belt around the mutt's neck and took him for a walk. It seemed to be a gentle canine. They walked in the grass and the 'pup' relieved himself. They returned to the airplane. Now that animal was sufficiently big and heavy that returning it to the cage was not a one-man job. He summoned help.

The second ramp agent climbed into the cargo compartment to facilitate recaging the 'dog.'

"OH MY GOD!" he exclaimed. "That's a WOLF en route to the Chicago Zoo!"

=====

On a Boeing 727 flight they had a Overheat on one air conditioning system. That's not a problem. It can be shut down and the Cargo Heat Switch closed to conserve pressurization. The Cargo Heat is exhausted air from the cabin.

The flight engineer mentioned to the Captain: "On the walk-around, I swear we had quite a few dogs in the forward cargo compartment."

An inquiry in the cabin determined that not only was that correct, but they were awesomely expensive show dogs. With no heat at that altitude, their days 'of show' were limited.

The Captain coordinated with ATC for a quick descent and clearance to an airport to protect the dogs. He did so successfully.

The following week he received a Letter of Commendation for his decisiveness that protected the airline's liability and image. In the same mail was his Letter of Reprimand for "Landing Overweight without a *bona fide* emergency." The FAA: "We do not land overweight for the protection of dogs." Lawdy, those planes could land massively overweight IF the touchdown was gentle and not abrupt.

≡ ═ ≡

Don't you love it at the airport when you're asked, "Has anyone unknown to you given you anything to transport?"

My answer: "I don't know anyone unknown to me."

"Has anyone, unknown to you, placed anything in your luggage?"

"How could I possibly know if it was an unknown action?" (Of course, you'd better hasten to just say "No.")

You saw it here first !!

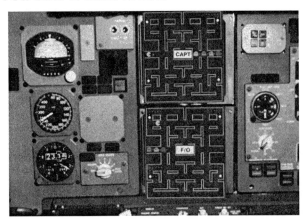

MAYDAY ON THE TAXIWAY

In the late 1980s my pal, Captain Wally Roberts, was taxiing a Boeing 727 at O'Hare-Chicago. Wally has been a close friend for many decades, an abruptly forthright man, but also a man saturated with good humor, generosity and a big heart. I am proud to call him a treasured friend to this day.

It was a clear night, visibility unlimited. One particular taxiway (called "the outer" in those days) was a lengthy stretch of cement from which there was entry and exit, but no turn-offs along its length. As they committed to the taxiway, they noticed another Boeing 727 on the same cement, coming in the opposite direction. Remember that there is no turn-off for either plane.

Wally inquired: "Wasn't TWA cleared to taxi south via the outer?"

ATC: "Yes you were." No further answer.

Wally: "Well it sure looks like there is another aircraft headed towards us."

ATC (after a pause): "A _____ 727 on the *other* ground control frequency has taken a wrong turn."

Wally: "If I recall the layout of this taxi way there is no place for either of us to exit or turn around between our respective positions."

ATC: "That is correct, but _____ says he can turn around and is now attempting to do so."

Captain Roberts watched this airplane continue to approach his position, swerving left and right, attempting to turn, giving up, judging distance, but still progressing toward an ultimate impact if not stopped (or turned).

Wally: "It is the consensus of this crew that a 727-200 cannot be turned around on this taxiway without going into the dirt."

ATC: No response.

They watched the 727 continue to advance, rather a drugged-looking stagger left and right, still contemplating the turn…BUT closing with the TWA aircraft. Someone had to stop. One plane or the other was getting a time-consuming reverse-push and it wasn't going to be Wally. Now the proximity was getting intimidating.

Wally: "Ground, why don't you stop this _____ 727 before impact?"

ATC: "Go to the other ground control frequency with that request."

Wally: "Ground control movements on taxiways is your job, not mine. Get him stopped."

This was becoming critical enough that Wally summoned a flight attendant and told her to think evacuation if impact became imminent. Now the airplane was less than 200 feet from TWA despite the landing lights Wally turned on to signal the urgency of the closure and his position.

Wally: "Is O'Hare ATC going to stop this fiasco?"

No reply. To his crew: "Watch this."

Wally: "Mayday-Mayday-Mayday! A ground collision between two passenger-carrying aircraft is imminent due to failure of ATC to provide safe control of taxiing traffic."

With that the other airplane stopped (never on the same frequency).

ATC Supervisor: "Thanks a lot, TWA. You've just shut down the entire airport!"

Wally: "And what choice did I have after ten minutes of pleading with you people to do your job with safety?"

No comment.

A tug arrived to reverse-taxi the intruding airplane. All three TWA crewmembers wrote Flight Debriefs on the incident, including one written by Wally: "Pilot's Use of Emergency Authority."

Wally heard nothing further until intercepting the V.P. of Flight Operations: "You did what you had to do, and it resulted in the tower taking a lot of heat. Good job."

Remember the Pilot-In-Command has the total responsibility and ultimate authority for the safe operation of the aircraft. Wally was never timid in exercising that responsibility and authority. I miss our encounters and fun in the ramp office.

The Cabin and the Flight Attendants In It

The most difficult positions on an airline are claimed by flight attendants and gate agents. With the problems and difficult passengers they endure, I would happily load bags or empty lavatories before attempting their job. The flight attendants and pilots exchange lots of needling jabs and jokes about one another, but there is harmony on a flight and teamwork. Flight attendants deserve an honorary degree in Psychology and Public Relations for the problems they solve with skill. I admire them, but still…a lot of funny things happened.

It's not the Captain who has power on the airplane—the flight attendants control the peanuts! As a passenger, when they hand me that tiny bag with six peanuts in it, I'm prone to say, "I couldn't possibly eat all of these. Do you have a doggie bag?"

Most new flight attendants are naïve, inexperienced and in a totally new environment. Therefore they are vulnerable. It is not true of the new hire flight attendant that "she was so dumb the other three Flight Attendants noticed!" or that "I blew in her ear and she thanked me for the refill." The new hires, however, are available victims.

===

The older flight attendants, when they were new hires, might have initially proclaimed, "I love to travel; love to see new places and shop; like people and always wanted to serve peanuts."

One of them told me many years later, "Look, pal, I've been on my feet for years, my White Knight has never arrived, and I've sold out my life for free travel to places I can't afford to go. You ask how I am?"

The more experienced flight attendants know how to avenge themselves on a caustic, abusive and ungentlemanly captain: Visine. In a way, they help him to see things better. This colorless, odorless and tasteless medication, with four or five drops injected into a cup of coffee, runs through the intestinal tract faster than an Olympian in the hundred-yard dash. In fact, 'dash' becomes the operative verb.

The flight attendants might offer the following perspective of pilots:

What's the difference between an airline captain and a jet engine?

The jet engine quits whining at the gate.

What separates the flight attendants from the lowest form of life on earth?

The cockpit door.

The tall, blonde, new hire flight attendant came to the cockpit as we flew over Iowa.

"What's that river down there?"

"Why," I replied, "that is the Euphrates."

She thanked me and turned to exit the cockpit.

"Wait a minute, sweetheart. See that other river up there? This one is the Euphrates and that one is the Tiber."

She thanked me again.

I remarked to the first officer, "Do you believe that! It's grade school geography."

A few moments later she knocked on the door. I clicked it open. The passengers were laughing hysterically. She had announced exactly those identities on the public address system. "Damn you!" she muttered and kicked the door closed.

=== === ===

Over the years the flight attendants became so young! One young lady delivered to me an unusually nice crew meal. I said, "This is splendid. Where were you when I was looking for a wife?"

She smiled, "I was probably in my crib, Captain."

=== === ===

So very young! Leaving Madison, Wisconsin the young flight attendant came to the cockpit. "We have a lady in first class whom I suppose I'm expected to know and treat special. Have you ever heard of Cyd Charisse?" I ventured back for a cup of coffee, actually to look at The Cyd. Let me assure you that to this day she has magnificent legs and is still beautiful.

=== === ===

One other incident is memorable. I'll camouflage the passenger's identity. The very young lady (perhaps 10 years of age) was one of the daughters in a family sitcom on TV. She was, as were all the characters, African-

American. The first class flight attendant was also and began introducing herself to the customers. As she arrived at this seat, she said, "I'm Charlotte. I've always known you as Ruthy. How shall I address you?"

The little twerp turned to her adult companion and said, "Will you tell *this woman* that she can address me as Miss Insolent-Tug'em and she can speak with you, not me." (Obviously I've altered the name).

═ ═ ═

The new hires were subject to time-worn games. On the Boeing 727 to the aft of the center pedestal is a small lever, the gear warning horn. It alerts the crew when the throttles are retarded to idle and the gear is not down. The flight engineer silences it, especially when descending from altitude or slowing down when gear is not a consideration.

The flight attendant was summoned to the cockpit. "We see in the maintenance logbook that the flushing motors in the lavatories are inoperative. We will have to use the manual flush procedures. Since we can't see back there, you will have to come up here and flush the toilets. It is this lever (gear warning horn)."

She made about forty trips to the cockpit on that leg, pulled the lever (to no genuine effect) and we thanked her effusively.

═ ═ ═

One of my friends on another carrier told a new hire flight attendant that they were an Environmental Protection Agency target flight. They would need air samples. She was to take a sick sack, scoop air into it when alerted, and seal it carefully. When she brought it to the cockpit they gave her the information to write on the bag: Date-Time-Altitude-Geographic location. In that leg they acquired about ten semi-inflated and well-identified sick sacks. Of course they left them for the next crew to puzzle over their value.

━━━

One of my Canadian friends was flying for a regional carrier up there. A new flight attendant visited the cockpit before departure. She was asking questions and noticed the three green lights above the gear handle. "Well, those tell us the gear is down and locked for landing."

En route they took out one of the bulbs. Upon gear extension they called her to the cockpit and told her, "We have a problem. The left main gear isn't down. You'll have to go back, mid-wing, and jump up and down four times on the floor."

While she did so, they reinserted the light bulb. She came to the cockpit and felt relief that she had contributed to safety. In fact, they allowed her to do so for the next six legs.

━━━

The captain sets the atmosphere with the crew virtually the moment he steps on the plane. When he barks "Black coffee" and retreats to the cockpit, it is not a harmonious beginning. However, when he introduces himself to each flight attendant, asks about their supplies, briefs them on the flight and assures them of his support with any problem, it builds teamwork. Sadly, some captains isolate that cockpit from the passenger compartment and will not enter the latter, despite the problems with passengers the flight attendant may be having.

The flight my memory summons had a rock star in First Class. I'd never heard of him, had not the least interest in him and never tried to gain any knowledge of his awesome talents. Once at altitude the star went to the coach section and invited one of his staff to join him in First Class, a violation of CAB regulations.

The flight attendant tried to explain that this was not permissible. "Do you know who I am?" our star snapped. She admitted she did. "Then get out of my face!" he snarled with venom.

She came to the cockpit angry, embarrassed in front of other passengers and even a bit tearful at being victim to such shabby treatment.

"What seat is he in?" I asked.

"The star is in 3-D and his friend is now in 3-E."

I left the cockpit with no hat, no tie, shirt collar wide open and slammed the cockpit door open. The echo of that reached about Row 22. Star and I exchanged the following:

Me (leaning over him, speaking to his invited friend): "I want you out of that seat and behind that curtain right now."

Star: "It's okay."

Me: "No, it will be okay when that seat is vacant. Get out of it *now!*"

Star: "Do you know who I am?"

Me: "Yes, you are the man who is leaving this airplane in handcuffs if you speak one more word to me. Do you know who I am?"

Our first class passengers were snickering and rewarded to see this pompous ass demeaned. His friend was out of that seat at Mach 2 speed. I received the best crew meals of my career on that leg.

≡ ≡

Supposedly we had another 'star' in First Class once who snapped the same response: "Do you know who I am?"

The flight attendant went forward, picked up the P.A. , and announced: "We have a gentlemen in First Class who does not know his identity. If anyone on board might help him and us, we'd be grateful."

≡ ≡

Out of ORD, a F/A supervisor got on to give the flight attendants a checkride.

The 737 had a siren on the autopilot disconnect that sounded like a French ambulance coming down the aisle and there is nothing you can do to silence it. As we were descending into BUF the very gentle, sensitive male flight attendant came to the cockpit and was complaining about the F/A supervisor as only one of his social sensitivity could do.

He said with a distinct lisp, "She has no more personality than this circuit breaker," at which point he touched a CB with his pen. I clicked off the autopilot and the racket began. At the same time I rolled into a steep

bank and yelled, "Oh my God!! Don't touch that one!"
Thought he was going to convulse or cry.

—Thanks to Tom Travis–American (Retired)

Within the 1990s the topic of sexual harassment soared
as an issue. We learned, amazingly enough, the average age
of a sexual harassment complaining flight attendant was 20
to 28 years old. (I think that is the same group that
considers Beavis and Butthead, the movie *Basic Instinct*
and Andrew 'Dice' Clay as class entertainment.) The more
mature flight attendants knew long ago how to deflect
unwanted attention and had comebacks sharp as a saber.

My crew briefing often included: "Prior to this trip I
visited the Chief Pilot. I have officially and irrevocably
surrendered my rights under the sexual harassment laws of
this country. If I have to get molested for a cup of coffee or
sell my body for a crew meal, I will not report any of you.
Do not feel threatened when you come to the cockpit. You
are all invited to my nude pool party at the hotel on
layover. If it is too late, too crowded, too cold, too windy,
or you are simply uncomfortable, we'll have it in the
shower in my room.'

(I quit that when one of the most overweight and
unattractive flight attendants I'd ever seen, passed by me in
leaving, nudged me, and said, "You'd better not be kidding
about that pool party next time." Gasp!)

I was also prone to say: "When I rip off this shirt, I look
like Schwarzenegger." (pause…contemplative look) "No, I
mean Schwarzkopf. It's one of those Germans."

A friend told me about an aggressive and socially ignorant Check Airman on another carrier. Loudmouthed and insensitive. The African-American flight attendant came to the cockpit to see if they'd like coffee.

Loudmouth: "I like my coffee like I like my women."

She is supposed to ask how: "Black, hot and sweet." She retorted instead, "We don't have any stupid coffee, Captain."

＝　＝　＝

That reminds me of sitting at the gate, awaiting departure. The flight attendant was in the cockpit and we watched drizzling rain hit the windshield. I remarked, "This reminds me of the first time I ever made love."

She exclaimed: "In the rain?"

I replied, "No, it was in the shower at a Ramada Inn."

＝　＝　＝

Traveling to the West Coast, the flight attendant came to the cockpit to tell me a highly agitated passenger wanted to see the captain. When I found him, he said, "How do you expect to clear the Rocky Mountains at 7000 feet of altitude?"

I said, "Well, if we were at 7000 feet, we surely wouldn't."

He held up his Casio watch, with altimeter, and advised me that we *were* at 7000 feet. I was caused to explain the difference between aircraft cruising altitude and cabin pressurized altitude. He howled with laughter at his misunderstanding.

＝　＝　＝

I had a lot of fun with passengers when using the public address system: "Ladies and gentlemen, the reason for this delay is that the machine that we use to break your luggage is inoperative. We have to do it by hand and it takes time."

=====

Gate agents deal often with aggressive, even abusive passengers. One passenger on check-in said, "I want this bag to go to Seattle, this one to go to Miami and the third to go to Dallas."

Of course she replied, "We can't do that!"

"Well," he snapped, "you did it last week!"

=====

"We are at 35,000 feet and still operating on a 97.2% confidence level that we can find Chicago."

When we arrived: "We found Chicago. It was within 87 miles of where we expected to find it. We're pretty excited about that navigational accuracy."

=====

"We are in takeoff position. In a moment we will charge down that runway faster than a speeding bullet, with more power than a locomotive and leap over all those buildings with a single bound. Yes, it is me: SuperCaptain."

=====

"Off to the left you can see the city of Chicago…or perhaps, Oklahoma City. We'll be landing to the south, which is exhilarating if you are one of those southbound landing fans. I expect to make an utterly velvet-smooth landing. If, however, it is rough or bounces, you'll know I turned it over to the copilot at the last moment for his experience and training."

=== === ===

(Spoken quietly): "Those of you on the right side of the airplane have a splendid view of Chicago. Do not everyone look at once! The people on the left side have nothing to look at. They'll know you have something to see. If I wanted them to see Chicago, I'd turn around."

=== === ===

On my retirement trip: "This is my last leg as an airline captain. All of the booze on the airplane is free. If you are in First Class, where it is free anyway, please take as a gift the seat you're in and the flight attendant of your choice."

=== === ===

One passenger in First Class summoned the flight attendant to complain: "This is really a bad steak! Can I have another?"

She took the plate, returned to the galley and the passengers could hear her 'spanking' the steak (actually, the counter) and saying, "Bad steak! Bad steak! You behave yourself!"

=== === ===

When I was assigned to San Francisco in 1978, it was quite a cultural change for a Midwestern lad. I was a bit astounded at the openness of the gay community and how patronized they were politically, financially, in newspapers and TV ads, etc.

On one flight the captain asked me how I liked San Fran. "Well, I guess I'm not accustomed to the populace of the homosexual community, 40% of the San Fran total citizens in one report, and how much appeal is made to them on TV and in the papers."

At the rear of the cockpit a rather sour, senior flight attendant was listening and remarked, "Well…40%. Does that apply to our pilots too?"

The Captain turned and looked at her solemnly: "Speaking for myself, sweetie, it would depend upon whether YOU were the option."

In the days of the Boeing 707 the cockpit was spacious. The flight engineer sat well aft of the pilots. One night the captain told a new hire flight attendant to look up through the overhead window. The planet Venus was sparkling mightily.

"That is the space shuttle, sweetheart."

"Really!?"

"Sure, you want to talk to them?"

"Can I?"

The captain put his microphone and audio selector on interphone and handed the headset and microphone to her. At the same time the flight engineer switched to interphone.

"What do I say to them?"

"Just say 'Hi, Space Shuttle'."

She did.

Answer: "Hello. Who is this?" replied the flight engineer in her earphones.

"Tell them you are TWA and you're over Pittsburgh."

She did.

"Well, we can't see you down there. Can you turn on your landing lights?"

The Captain flipped a couple of switches.

"Yes, we see you now. We're busy, but have a good evening."

That little chick told everyone on the airplane, many with puzzled expressions, that she had been talking to the space shuttle from the cockpit.

All the flight attendants were gathered for the typical preflight briefing for a 747 flight to Honolulu. Once they'd discussed the passenger load, meal and beverage service, length of trip and layover, a new hire flight attendant raised her hand to ask, "Do we get a sheet on the currency conversion and exchange rate?" (Hawaii is a state within the United States, in case you too have forgotten.)

Supposedly a flight attendant announced, "Well, try to compose yourself after that landing while Captain Kangaroo bounces us to the terminal building."

Southwest Airlines has a few announcements that are creative:

"The seat belt buckles like any seat belt, including the one in your car. If you do not know how to buckle a seat belt, perhaps you should not be out in public."

"In the case of cabin pressure loss, quit screaming, grab the oxygen mask in front of you, put it on and breathe normally. Yeah, right! If you have a child or someone acting like a child beside you, put on your mask first and then the child's. If you have two children, decide now which one you like best."

━━━

Another Southwest announcement that gave me a chuckle: "There may be fifty ways to leave your lover, but there are only four ways out of this airplane. Please pay attention to the evacuation safety direction."

━━━

One flight attendant had a cute quip if it hadn't been given to an Iowa politician. Landing in Des Moines the passenger asked: "Do we set our watches back an hour?"

She replied: "In Iowa I'd set it back a century."

━━━

I'd not like to have been the Captain of one of our major airlines, facing the flight attendants afterwards, when he announced: "Ladies and Gentlemen, we've reached cruising altitude and will be turning down the cabin lights. This is for your comfort and to enhance the appearance of your flight attendants."

━━━

We had one captain who really was a master of public address announcements. Great humor, creative. He would include, "In the back we have four of TWA's finest, most qualified flight attend...well, three out of four anyway. However, MaryAnn is trying her best."

He would conclude: "I was just kidding about MaryAnn. She is a mighty fine young lady." (Lady is pronounced, of course, "lay-dee.")

One day a flight attendant stormed in and told him, "If I were MaryAnn I'd have you reported to the Chief Pilot in a minute!" She slammed the door. He was baffled. He'd done this for years with no conflict. He summoned another attendant to the cockpit: "Did I offend MaryAnn in some way?"

"If you didn't, I'm amazed. That was so uncalled for, Captain." (She exited).

Finally he called MaryAnn to apologize. She was gracious. "Don't worry about it. We've been friends a long time."

Finally they reasoned out what the conflict might be. The airplane was powered by the APU (Aux Power Unit) while they started engines. During the course of his announcement the Flight Engineer transferred ship's power from the APU to an engine generator which *cut off the PA system*. It just so happened that killing the PA happened just as he was enunciating, "I was just kidding about MaryAnn. She's a mighty fine young lay…"

Leaving the cockpit to use the lav was miserable when you had to wait in line. As a pilot you had to nod to all the passengers, or if there was a big line, pretend you'd come back for a cup of coffee (rather than be absent from the cockpit for any length of time). We had two instances where this got funny.

On one flight we had a flight attendant continuously primping in the lav. She was always exiting with fresh makeup, new lipstick, perfume or some personal attention. The captain waited…and waited. He assumed it was her again. He slammed his hand against the wall of the lav, four or five times. Out came a timid, elderly little lady, with her head down and terrified.

━━━

On another flight the lav door seemed to be stuck. The captain pulled…and pulled again. Finally he snatched it open with all the strength he could muster…and pulled some little old lady right off the toilet. She didn't know how to lock the door and was holding it shut from the inside.

━━━

(Incidentally, when polled, 62% of all children reported, in a reversed role presence, they would probably not put an oxygen mask over their parent's face….just a grin. Not true.)

━━━

It was mealtime during a flight on El-Al. "Would you like dinner?" the flight attendant asked Moshe, seated in front.

"What are my choices?" Moshe asked.

"Yes or no," she replied.

Pass Privileges and No One Made a Pass

All airlines offer free travel, space available, for employees. It is ideal to learn the aircraft is lightly loaded and the pass rider is assured to travel. Then there is the full flight, even the oversold flight, where boarding is tenuous, stress is present and only at the last minute will the pass rider win or lose.

A flight attendant named Gay had registered to travel, validated his presence to board, and waited anxiously. About three minutes before departure the gate agent handed Gay a boarding pass and seat assignment and he hastened aboard. It happens often. Apparently two friends wished to sit side by side and changed seats, one of which had been assigned to Mr. Gay. Nonetheless, that vacated a seat, which the pass rider was still happy to find.

Within that three minutes the last passenger did, in fact, show up, making the aircraft fully occupied. All non-revenue passengers must be summoned from the plane.

The flight attendant walked to the seat assigned to flight attendant Gay (who is not in it) and asked somewhat brusquely, "Are you Gay?" The passenger blushed, twisted in his seat and somewhat frustrated, stated, "Well, yes. I am."

The flight attendant said: "Please get your carry-on luggage and come with me. You'll need to leave the plane."

Under any circumstances a non-rev would understand what was transpiring.

Our flight attendant Gay, however, overheard the exchange, stood up and said, "Hey, wait a minute. *I'm Gay.*"

A frustrated flight attendant, about to take a delay, said: "Well, both of you get your luggage and let's go to the jetway. Please hurry."

With this a third passenger stood and declared, "I'm gay, too. What kind of homophobic airline is this? You want me to come with you, too? I can't believe this is taking place!"

You can bet the flight attendant was feeling the same way.

The late TWA Captain Russ Day created these images that have been enjoyed over the years:

THE CAPTAIN
AS SEEN BY
HIMSELF

THE CAPTAIN
AS SEEN BY
PASSENGERS

THE CAPTAIN
AS SEEN BY
THE F.A.A.

THE CAPTAIN AS SEEN BY HIS WIFE

THE CAPTAIN AS SEEN BY THE HOSTESS

THE CAPTAIN AS SEEN BY THE COPILOT

SLOJ, OR THE OVAL COCKPIT

A speaker lost to memory once referred to SLOJ (an acronym you can pronounce, but it means Sudden Loss of Judgment). It explains many aircraft mishaps, presuming there existed judgment initially. This isn't it.

One international airline had a swinging 'wild and crazy guy' Captain, loved to party and had a healthy attraction to the chicks. In a bar he met either two attractive barmaids or two customers. The mutual affection was immediate. Let's call them Heidi and Monica.

He had a flight to Paris within the week, so why not invite them along? In that interval he could acquire employee discount tickets of token price for each of the lasses. He did so.

Somewhere over the North Atlantic (long before the terrorist days, but certainly after passengers could no longer visit the cockpit), he went back to visit with these good-looking hunks of fluff. What could be more impressive than inviting them to the cockpit?

As the three entered the first officer protested, "Hey, we can't do this. You can't invite passengers up here in flight." I'm sure the Captain, who after all is the Commander, silenced him abruptly and with an audience it was irresistible to prove who is in command. This is a thirty-days-on-the-beach offense, if not termination, so we have a mighty angry first officer. Even 'innocent,' no one wants a conflict with his captain in a disciplinary hearing.

When one of the females (Heidi) displayed her video camera and began taping, the first officer said, "That's it. I'm out of here. It's bad enough now without videotaped evidence that they were up here." He got up, the captain shrugged and the F/O left the cockpit. The autopilot was engaged, following the INS program, and no action would be required on such a lovely, smooth day of flight.

Our starring lady guest (Monica) immediately gets affectionate with the captain, rubbing his shoulders, a kiss on the cheek, hands reaching forward to rub his chest and we're progressing toward an orgy. This cockpit intern does not distract Heidi from her photojournalist assignment.

Soon the captain's seat is electrically driven rearward and Guest #1 (who we decided to call Monica) is honoring the Captain with such respect that you'd think 'Hail to the Chief' would be playing over the PA system. I have no idea what color dress she was wearing.

Heidi, of course, continues her assignment. A photojournalist is exposed to all scenarios, from the gory to uplifting and exciting news coverage.

All good things end in time. The ladies exited the cockpit (two-story-high 747, so their entry wasn't all that obvious to begin with) and a very displeased first officer returned to duty. No record is known of the conversation between the two crewmembers, but the flight continued without incident. On the return flight, however, some exchange must have occurred by which both women remained in their cabin coach seat. No return cockpit view.

Within a month the airline received a phone call, routed to the Legal Department, demanding $50,000 or the video (described for the receiving caller who had not viewed it) would be turned over to "Inside Edition" for nationwide TV coverage. Most certainly dynamite and a destructive public relations problem is ticking away toward detonation.

They made one mistake. To call the 'victim' (so to speak) and demand a price for not exposing violations of Federal Air Regulations, lewd and obscene conduct on a passenger flight, has a name: *extortion*. That's a criminal act in itself.

So in meeting to finalize the generous offer, the Legal Department (no doubt accompanied by the FBI, the police or some authority of intimidation) met with Heidi and Monica. As the story unfolded, the evidence revealed (and its location), the facts of law were explained to two naïve simpletons. No money exchanged hands. One tape did. Certifications of no existing copies were signed, and other materials to negate any influence with which two women entered the room.

Naïve? "Inside Edition" probably would have promptly paid that amount or more and kept their source anonymous. Whether they would have blurred out the Captain's face remains to be known. His future, however, was a certainty. Greyhound? Amtrak?

Sic transit gloria mundi: So goes the wonders of the world.

LEARNING NEWTON'S LAWS
AS PUBLISHED IN *PLANE AND PILOT* MAGAZINE
(2005)

O nce upon a time, I'd written an article about the growing popularity of hang gliders. The magazine wanted a picture of me flying one to accompany the article. I'd never touched one. Driving through Provo, Utah, I stopped once to watch hang gliders flying, climbing, virtually surfing the winds coming over one of the mountains. Beautiful sight!

There are laws of aerodynamics, thanks to Bernoulli. Newton gave us a few about gravity, and equal-and-opposite reactions. Newton said a body in motion would remain in motion until an opposing force intervened. There's always been the undefined, but oft-quoted law of common sense. Overconfident, ego-assured and overly aggressive are well understood in society, not requiring science.

The photographer and the hang glider dealer awaited me. The photographer was at the base of a small bluff, maybe 25 feet in height. The hang glider dealer had the craft assembled above. The setting sun made it urgent that the flight occur before darkness precluded photography.

Dual? Explanation? Suggestions? "Nope, a wing is a wing. They all fly the same. Strap it on me." The first photograph reveals me lying under a hang glider in a clump of bushes, pants torn, jacket ripped—the expression of pain was priceless.

There's another adage: In a time of stress, one will revert to the strongest habit pattern.

Let's envision flight control of hang gliders. Extend your hand, palm down and horizontal or parallel to the floor. Extend and place the index finger of the other hand where the fingers join the palm of the horizontal hand. Assume there are welded. Now raise the angle of attack to climb. Which way did the index finger move? You moved or pushed it forward. Push forward to climb, pull rearward to descend. That's pretty simple—different, but simple.

Flinging myself aloft on the first effort there had been, somehow, a ghastly dive toward the ground that promised pain. Instinct! Pull to climb. I've never attempted an outside loop before, but that's as close as any effort ever made.

"No. I'm fine. I've got it figured out. Let's go back up there." (Oh Lawd, no one can hurt this bad and actually be conscious!)

As a logical person, with a couple of thousand flight hours, and now only one crash on my resumé, I paused to think it out: To climb, one pushes forward; to descend, ya pull back. Push and the houses get smaller; pull and they get bigger. Repeating anything with sufficient repetition injects it firmly in the cranial cavity. "No, I've got it. No help needed. Everyone get ready."

On the second effort and immediately after launch, I was mentally void and mesmerized as a deer in headlights:

"Diving! I'm going to crash again! Pull back!" Oh, the pain! Now the knee is torn from my slacks, plus we have a little blood for color. And I'm mad. "Take it back up there. If I break it, I'll buy it. I've got it figured out now."

How simple. Focus on the tip of the glider. To go up, push the tip of the glider up. To go down (and let's not), pull the tip of the glider down. Forget your hands—move the tip of the glider. Lots of repetition, focused rehearsal with a few moments of sunlight left. Laughter is extremely distracting. It's amazing what some think is funny! Would you laugh at an injured man, clothes torn, multiple scratches and a little blood on cheek and knee? I'm working with two sadists. They, of course, are patronizing stupidity. The instructor even quoted me, but I don't recall smirking: "A wing is a wing. They all fly the same." Now devoid of compassion, he had no suggestions.

The third flight was a beauty. The photo shows me aloft (they airbrushed the photograph to camouflage the torn clothing). It is the image, the epitome of mastery of hang gliding by an experienced aviator.

Do not alter events that are progressing well. *The glide* had been mastered. Landing had not been considered. Simple: Just glide into whatever happens to be in the way and promises a stop. A body in motion stays in motion until some equal force precludes it. More bushes. One tree. More pain. There was a mission. We'd accomplished it.

The photographer confirmed we had a splendid aerial shot. The hang glider owner extracted his aircraft from under me (or over me—everything was rather fuzzy). They were so pleased with the outcome that it inculcated genuine laughter and happiness. Brightening someone's day is a warm feeling (or maybe that was the warmth of blood flow).

"Thanks for all your help, fellows. Perhaps I'll just lie here for a while and contemplate the sunset. Your concern is appreciated. This can't be arterial blood flow; don't worry about it. I enjoyed every minute of it. Let's cancel the article about parasailing. I'll substitute that idea with one about flying IFR in a Tetrahedron."

In one afternoon, I'd become Newton's apple and Bernoulli's disgust. Don't tell me there are no old, bold pilots. I am growing old, and was exceptionally bold.

Arriving home: "The photo shoot went fine. There was a street gang that attacked me on the way home, and there were just too many of them. Would you drive me to the nearest hospital?"

At the airport: "Oh, nonsense. You saw the photograph. I flew it marvelously. Some loudmouth photographer and instructor are creating for your benefit. When I heal the wounds from that dog attacking me, I'll deal with them. A wing is a wing. They all fly the same—you know that."

What'd I learn? First in times of stress, one reverts to the strongest habit pattern. Secondly, don't write about anything you haven't done. (If so, bring a Bible and make observers swear oaths of your choice.) Permit me a thirdly and fourthly: Bloodstains are difficult to remove and the body heals amazingly well. It was an educational afternoon. (With all of his unparalleled experience, Bill Cox never ferried a hang glider!)

The PA System: Public Assault
As published in *Plane and Pilot* Magazine
(2005)

Every airline has a Flight Operations Policy Manual. It's been amassed over the years to regulate everything from animals in the cabin, intoxicated passengers, operating procedures, conduct, dress codes and (sigh!) public address system announcements: the PA. Welcome passengers aboard; keep them advised of any delays; announce arrival weather; talk endlessly?

After everyone has endured gate agents and flight attendants endlessly welcoming us aboard, the cockpit gets enthusiastic: "We'd like to add our welcome aboard... And thanks for choosing Unctuous Airlines." (They were the cheapest price; that's why everyone chose this flight.)

Sometimes I'm playful. When they say, "In charge of your flight today is Captain Whizbang Shanks, assisted by First Officer Ace Travis..." I'll turn to my seatmate and say, "Wow. Those two do good work. I'm glad they're up there." Never heard of them! Won't see them. Why do I care? When they announce, "We'll be landing on Runway 29," I might comment, "Well, that's a smooth one. I'm glad they're using it."

Don't ya love it when it's pitch black outside and the captain announces, "Our route of flight will be over Peoria,

Milwaukee, Dallas, Chicago, then direct to Orlando." I don't care even when it's daylight. No one is listening. Shucks, as a captain I knew that. We are, however, trying to read! Any captain making a PA announcement after 10 p.m. and airborne ought to carry everyone's bags upon arrival.

Admittedly, I made PA announcements, too. "Ladies and gentlemen, in a moment we'll charge down that runway faster than a speeding bullet, with more power than a locomotive, and leap over all those buildings in a single bound. I just wanted you to know who is up here. Yes, it is Super Captain. Please prepare for takeoff." The job was supposed to be fun, as well as operated competently and with utmost safety.

"We're at 35,000 feet and still operating on a 97.2% confidence level that we can, in fact, find Chicago. If we do, the weather there is (whatever). I know you're enjoying the service of four of our finest flight attendants…well, three out of four, anyway."

Always enjoyed flying with First Officer Jean Preudhomme, native of France. Leaving Dallas, Jean would make a nonessential PA announcement in French, then I'd add, "I just wanted you Texans to know how much culture and couth we have in the cockpit today." (Crossing the Red River was "leaving the holy land.")

"Ladies and gentlemen, we are ecstatic on the flight deck. We found Chicago. It was within 85 miles of where we thought it would be. We're landing to the south, which is exciting if you're a southbound landing fan."

Virtually all of Chicago, out to the suburbs, is now lit in the new high-intensity amber streetlights. "On the left side of the airplane, you have a splendid view of Chicago, where they have now illuminated the high crime areas in the amber streetlights." (Got my hands spanked for that one.)

"As we arrive in St. Louis, you'll see the major sports triangle. There is Busch Memorial Stadium, home of the Cardinals. To the north is the domed home of the Rams, and then there is the big arch that commemorates the croquet tournaments we have in St. Louis." (A St. Louis city councilman told me: 'That's funny, but I wish you wouldn't say that again.')

Sometimes, quietly: "If you're on the left side of the airplane, you have a great view of Phoenix. Don't everyone look at once! The people on the right side will know they don't have anything to see. If I want them to see Phoenix, I'll turn around." That theme also worked this way: "If you look out the left side of the airplane, you'll see Omaha… well, it's Omaha or Tulsa. I'm not sure, but it's a big city."

The Hale-Bopp Comet was a real treat. Up at 35,000 or 37,000 feet MSL at night, we were all above the haze and contamination of civilization. I'd ask the flight attendants to turn off all the cabin lights and then get permission from ATC to do 360-degree turns. We had views of that comet that remain indescribable. Simply beautiful with that streaming tail behind it, against a pitch-black sky. It took about three or four full rotations, left and right, for everyone to see it. Those on the aisle had to lean over or change seats. We gave them time to do that. If we were a couple of minutes late, no one complained. They'd seen something to remember for a lifetime.

During daylight hours we'd point out the contrails of invisible airplanes to young flight attendants and advise, "That's the Hale-Bopp Comet up there." Sure it was— heading east and with a 200-mile cloud trail behind it. Sometimes there were two or three comets.

You are a captive audience, buckled in a seat and victim to whatever the captain wants to broadcast over the PA system. I cringe when the captain mentions "*my* copilot and *my* flight attendants." Unwarranted possession. I referred to whoever occupied the right seat as "my co-captain." He or she had better be. If anything disabled me, he/she *was the captain.*

There is one relay on a DC-9 that never breaks. When it does, the overhead speaker becomes a microphone. Don't ask me how. Our flight attendants were knocking on the door before takeoff: Prohibited! They were fervently pounding on the door after takeoff when I made an awesome, socially unacceptable, but humorous remark to the copilot. It transmitted over the PA. So advised, we pulled the PA circuit breaker. Upon arrival, not one passenger comment, except the little old lady who said, "Shame on you." What could I say? "Yes ma'am, I've already reprimanded him severely."

Up and Away....In My Hot Air Balloon
As published in *Plane and Pilot* Magazine
(2004)

The 1960s was a Golden Decade in aviation. There were pilot shortages; massive airline hiring and pilot training was overwhelming. My fellow instructors and I got into a *ratings race*, collecting licenses. For some reason, as the FAA created the balloon licensing requirements, they were willing to 'grandfather' anyone with a hot air balloon license freely and upon request. I didn't. If I hadn't flown it, I didn't want it on my license.

All of us were Instrument Instructors, multi-engine rated and most of us had Airline Transport Pilot licenses when the Veteran's Education Benefit bill included flight training. If a student had a private license, he or she could continue through all of the ratings, paying only 10% of the costs. It really was a farce of government expense. Many who couldn't get a job pumping gasoline were spending thousands of dollars getting pilot's licenses. On the other hand, many who couldn't afford a dream were able to pursue it.

Having all the needed ratings, the VA Bill opened up for us (in our ratings race) many adventures. I was now rated in gyroplanes, helicopters, seaplanes and gliders. With concurrent Instructor ratings I actually did get some employment and income from those vehicles. That still left the hot air balloon. While not covered by the GI Bill, it remained a challenge.

Also, at the Smithsonian Air and Space Museum there is an admirable display of the Double Eagle II, the balloon that crossed the Atlantic in 1978 with Maxie Anderson, Ben Abruzzo and Larry Newman. Maxie and I were at Missouri Military Academy together. He was a senior; I was an eighth grader. He was hero material even then. Maxie and Don Ida were killed in a balloon race in 1983 when drifting into communist territory. They landed, pulled the mechanical disconnects from the balloon, and they did not function. Sadly and aloft again, about 200 feet above the ground, those disconnects did operate. They tumbled to their deaths. Ben was killed in an airplane sometime later. Nonetheless, I wanted to fly a balloon.

Finding the equipment and an instructor was not a difficult challenge, but admitting acrophobia was more than I was willing to expose. Tall ladders are dizzying to me. I can't look over balconies into the lobby of hotels when I'm on the top floors. Ferris wheels and roller coasters? Fergitaboutit. In an aircraft my feet are on the floor and I'm contained, in control. It's amazed me how many other airline pilots have this fear of heights.

If you've ever complained about the time to preflight an airline, you need to prepare a balloon for flight. It must be carried from its transport, unfolded, unrolled, spread out, unwrinkled and then inflation begins with a big, *big* fan. It is, of course, attached to the basket where the pilots ride.

This is a lengthy task, pushing out wrinkles and opening the balloon sufficiently to introduce heat.

Once that critter is heat-filled, it lifts vertically above the basket (which is tied down, weighted down or held down at this point). The two of us climbed on board.

The first three flights were fascinating. So quiet. The ability to talk to people on the ground. Once, the winds were a bit more than we estimated and we almost skimmed a power line in departure. Another time in landing we were drug along the ground in the basket more than I enjoyed. All in all, I can understand the fascination of hot air balloon aviators. It's quiet, serene and the view is superb.

I didn't mind looking out, that's to say, *horizontally*. Looking down was no joy to me. Always lingering in my mind was that one had to fly this balloon *solo* to 5000 feet AGL for the commercial rating. You're not even permitted to substitute five root canals to avoid it.

At about 3000 feet above the ground, my instructor pointed out how to view the horizon to maintain altitude. "Do you see we are sinking? Try to add enough heat to maintain altitude." This was a single-burner unit. When I pulled for flame/heat, it sounded like *fut!* (pronounced explosively) as it *flamed out.* No heat. We're cooling and going down over a residential area.

"Ah, what do we do now?" The instructor pulled out a spark-striker, like any propane igniter, *leaped up on the edge of the basket* and relit the flame. Two human feet, balanced on a four-inch edge, hanging onto the risers and 3000 feet above the ground. This alone exposed that Mrs. Gwinn's son was a devout coward and his balloon career was over. Ain't no way, ever, that I'm climbing *to stand* on the edge of that basket. If it flames out, it's going down! (Modern balloons have dual burners to preclude this problem, so don't permit this to poison your perspective of hot air balloon aviation.)

I'm cool. I cried only a little bit in overwhelming admiration and the emotional joy of my instructor's skill. The rest of the flight was eternal. We couldn't get on the ground fast enough in my view. Being drug along the ground in the basket was pure joy because our altitude was about six inches. The instructor pulled out the heat escape panel in the top of the balloon to deflate it. There was no doubt in my aeronautical mind that "Balloon-Hot Air" would *never* decorate my pilot's license.

It's not over. The chase vehicle has to find you. Then the balloon must be disconnected, folded and rolled with focused attention, and a heavy bundle carried to the trailer. Five thousand feet SOLO—No way. Relighting that burner—Never!

"That was great. I'll call you for my next lesson." (On the same day that Madonna enters a convent.)

"Hot air balloons? Oh yeah, I've got five hours in them. I just didn't the time to finish the rating and my instructor moved." I can still get a tear in both eyes thinking about that relight and me (never) doing it.

ROUGH BEGINNING, GOOD ENDING

Every so often there was a Captain with whom you could not bond in any fraternity of the cockpit. As a new engineer I encountered Bill. We later became good friends. I was to learn also that he'd recently lost his wife and was living in isolation on a boat. That certainly gave me grief to have condemned him so readily with our first encounter. He later died a terrible death from cancer.

Even on the Boeing 707 the flight engineer's job was boring to me. I always sought out something simply *to do*. Whoever was flying the leg, the other pilot communicated. So as the Captain flew, I slid my seat forward and changed frequencies for the first officer. He could simply flip the switch to the new frequency. A real convenience. The Captain watched me do this on the first leg and without comment.

Our first conflict came on the first officer's (second) leg. When the Captain was given a frequency change, I began to dial it for him. He *slapped* my hand off the radio control panel. Not a word spoken. I retreated.

Later a flight attendant brought the superb first class luxuries (which we used to have) to the cockpit: grapes, cheese, crackers and some orange juice. As she set it on my desk I remarked, "Ah, this is right out of Arabian Nights."

The Captain began to punch me on the shoulder, "What are you two talking about?!"

My patience was eroding, "Absolutely nothing about this flight, the safety of it, or you, Captain." He returned to sulking.

As we secured the cockpit in Delaware, I handed the aircraft logbook to the captain for his signature. That he was watching me via peripheral vision was apparent. He signed the book and *threw* it over his shoulder, striking the panel, then me. I got up, put on my coat and secured my flight bag. Then I picked up the logbook from the floor, patiently smoothed and refolded all the pages and closed the cover. Then I snarled, "&*%$ *#$@!" and hurled it into the corner of the cockpit. I left the airplane.

As the first officer and I walked to dinner, he inquired, "What's going on with you and the Captain?"

I confessed that I had no idea, but, "I've about had it, whatever the cost."

We entered the dining room through the bar where our Captain sat with an empty glass and a fresh beverage. Long layover, no big deal. "Hey, here's my crew! Come on over here, guys. I'd like to buy you a drink. What'll you have, Kirk? ('a beer') What would you like, Dave?"

I said; "Nothing, Captain. I think it's against the Flight Operations Policy manual to drink on layovers. I think it's a rather insignificant comfort if you lose your job to enjoy it. Thank you anyway." I walked abruptly into the restaurant.

When Kirk joined me, he remarked, "My gawd, you just about put him into convulsions with that comment."

I replied, "I had to walk off because I was suppressing laughter. Really nailed him, didn't I? There's no way I'm ordering a beer now."

The Captain was effusively kind to me the next day. He even offered me the choice of crew meals. (And as I said, we became good friends as the years passed. I remember him and the initial conflict with affection.)

———

Roy was the talk of the domicile. In the right seat and among his contemporaries in the ramp office, he was a genuinely nice guy. Once in that left seat he was a raging, demanding, critical tyrant. He'd yelled at baggage handlers, gate agents, even demanded that a flight attendant "get your suitcase and get off this airplane. You're off the flight."

No counseling affected Roy. He could always present some paragraph of the Flight Ops Policy manual to justify what he'd done. Copilots avoided him. Flight attendants moaned upon boarding and finding him in the cockpit. 'Maniac' became the identity. He wasn't a bad pilot nor did he conduct a bad flight; he simply couldn't get along with anyone once he occupied the left seat.

The chief pilot was a good friend and bemoaned the problems he had with Roy. I said: "Fire him. If he sues, it will take ten years to get it into court with the battery of lawyers you have. If this airline makes it, as you think it will, then you'll have the money to pay him off. If it doesn't, it's a moot issue." The boss was perplexed and stymied about what to do with Roy. He was demoted to the right seat for six months, became a fine first officer and then reverted to rogue when restored to power.

The conclusion to the story came in some small Midwestern layover station. Roy had a scene with another flight attendant, expelling her from the flight. The other three flight attendants anticipated a conflict, reached agreement earlier and also picked up their bags to leave the airplane. "Where are you three going?"

One replied, "We've had it with you, Captain. Find yourself another cabin crew."

Roy stormed into the cockpit. "Get Scheduling on the horn. I need to get another cabin crew."

The first officer had already packed his flight bag, stood up and said, "Get a first officer, too, Roy. I'm fed up with you as well." Within two minutes Roy was in command of an empty cockpit and empty airplane.

He was eventually terminated. No one ever understood what flaw turned an often-exposed nice guy into such a varmint.

━━━━

We had another very hyper captain, actually a nice guy, whose driven personality simply grated on the nerves of gate agents, mechanics and baggage loaders. One day he was jumpseating to his home base of Chicago (riding in the cockpit on the extra seat), and put his suitcase by the forward cargo bin for it to be loaded. When the baggage loaders saw HIS name on it, they laid it down and backed the belt loader (several tons in weight) over it a dozen times.

When he retrieved it in Chicago, he came to the cockpit with dazed eyes, a suitcase about two inches thick and said, "Look what they did to my bag!" You couldn't have put two shirts in that suitcase. I'm sure our howls of hilarity didn't pacify his genuinely hurt feelings.

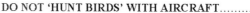

DO NOT 'HUNT BIRDS' WITH AIRCRAFT.........

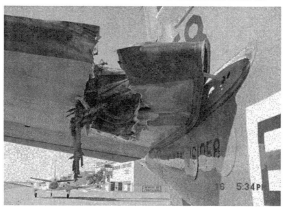

ASSESSING PILOT SKILLS

AS PUBLISHED IN *PLANE & PILOT* MAGAZINE (2002)

Occasionally my email has a psychological nuance: "What characteristics do you see in superior professional pilots?" In traveling the world, lecturing to airline, corporate and military aviators, those I'd classify as obviously superior had one arm longer than the other; they wear big, heavy watches. Shirt size: 16-inch collar and right-left sleeves 33 and 36 inches, respectively.

In class there is an arm raised, begging a question, and I see a watch thereon. This person must be ignored. A real pilot can't raise the arm on which a bona fide aviation watch is worn. Therefore, this would-be inquiry originates with someone wearing a *little watch* and with not enough pride to hide it in public. General George Patton probably would have slapped him and demanded his exit from 'this group of honorable men.'

At the beginning of my airline tenure, one invested three months' income in an appropriate watch. You couldn't read those little dials (and probably couldn't remember what they did), but it was requisite for the job. Someone may have had a technical question about fuel burn, time en route or weight and balance. On some watches you could spin the E6B computer circling the rim of the watch face, hesitate long enough to dream up an answer, and announce an answer with strong affirmation. Around non-pilots one could pause, contemplate some unspoken issue, consult and spin the watch bezel, nod and appear satisfied: "Never mind, it was just an aviation calculation that I've pondered." Class act!

One company manufactured a watch with a rotating compass-bezel on the rim. I noted my path always seemed to be North. (Hence, you had to find moss on a tree to orient it. In the airplane and once set, however, you found that you'd held the course without flaw or effort.) Another watch had an altitude pressure sensor within it. A would-be-helpful pilot as a passenger summoned me from the cockpit to inquire how I expected to clear the Rockies at 7000 feet MSL. He pointed to his pressure-sensitive watch. "We're in a pressurized airplane. Cabin pressure is about 7000 feet; aircraft altitude is 33,000."

Back in the Golden Days we had standards and values. Could you drive a nail with your watch? Was it included in the weight and balance calculations of the airplane? Could you move from seat-to-seat in the rear of an airliner and note the pilot had to retrim the airplane? Does the Mastercard payment on your watch equal your car payment? Could you use it as a mace in an altercation? Were your biceps asymmetrical? One called it: Pride!

Now days I've seen (gasp) Casio and Timex watches that no one would have worn on the ramp, even loading baggage in the romantic days of aviation. It is immaterial that some of us consult such people for "What day of the week is it?" since a Rolex GMT-Master has only the date.

Digital watches were a fad for a while. No youngster knew what "a quarter to four" meant with one of those. ATC might announce "Traffic at six o'clock"; they'd stare at their digital watch in confusion. They might mumble: "I think we'll be landed and at the gate by six o'clock. These ATC guys are extremely cautious."

My own timepiece is a stainless steel Rolex GMT-Master. My pal Barry Schiff has a solid gold model of the same watch. I have accused him of buying a Hawaiian knock-off for $25, but then observed that he had one arm four inches longer than the other. That's validation. His gold watch scratches easy and it's ostentatious. Honoring decades of friendship I volunteered to exchange watches with him. His pathetic excuse in refusing is long forgotten. (Buy a $25 'solid-gold' knockoff! When you feel the impact just before unconsciousness on a dark street in some big city you know you're not going to lose anything of value. Barry has the courage to be assaulted for *the genuine item*.)

Wearing a Rolex you know you're simply admired. You stand out in the crowd. Admirers in Manhattan, the Panama Canal Zone and Honduras have followed me. I think they just wanted to get close enough to *be seen* with someone wearing a Rolex. I stayed in well-lit areas so that fraternity could be observed. They didn't appear to be pilots, but they knew watches.

Perhaps FAA Examiners should be additionally certified as WAPs (Watch Authorization Pilots). We could designate an array of watches approved for private pilots and subsequent ratings or wristwatches awarded for proficiency. I could have authorized Mickey Mouse watches to three student pilots (now licensed) who come to mind. When renting an airplane you might hear, "Let me see your pilot's certificate, medical certificate and wristwatch, please." In fact, let's begin to name aircraft by the pilot-wristwatch skill required to fly them: Cessna Citizen, Piper Pulsar, Mooney Omega or perhaps a high-performance Beechcraft Rolex.

The astronauts were originally given watches with a 24-hour face on them. All 24 hours of the day in a circle. They hated them. After a long meeting one asked the moderator: "What time is it?" When he looked at his genuine astronaut watch like a fawn stunned in headlights, they all unstrapped the watches and left them on the table. I've seen those watches. If they were two inches bigger in diameter, they might have been acceptable.

I've read that the first two attempts by the Wright Brothers were defeated by the weight of the watch worn by the one flying. There was tradition before there were airplanes. I found a basic, strap-on, uncomplicated watch in Munich, Germany. It was, however, wider than a credit card is vertically: Gotta have that one!

After growing up in a military school, then the Army and airlines, time is rather an obsession with me. I'd rather be thirty minutes early for any appointment than two minutes late. I've not found that perfect wristwatch. My wife inventoried those of mine and told me two of the twelve need new batteries. The others are just misplaced around the house, I guess.

COWBOY BILL: ONE OF MY FAVORITE MEMORIES
AS PUBLISHED IN *PLANE & PILOT* MAGAZINE (2000)

I've been writing the book *Airways and Airwaves: Stories I Tell To Friends*. It's an assembly of all the hilarious events in a long aviation and airline career. It has been great reverie to edit those that are belly-chuckle amusing from those more complicated and hysterical. One of my all-time favorite general aviation memories has been Bill.

Bill, no doubt, remains a prominent lawyer in the lower Southwest. He's big, loud, fun, with a gift of Western metaphor in his speech that can tickle your type rating. Bill wears handmade, self-designed cowboy boots, Eisenhower jackets of mink and plush Stetson cowboy hats that are awesomely handsome. Bill is a striking presence. Look up the word 'flamboyant' and you find not only Bill's photo, but also a soundtrack to keep you laughing.

Bill had two law offices, one in 'Cowpoke' (identity camouflaged) and one in 'Cowtown,' about 100 miles apart. He decided the easiest, fastest way to commute between the two was to acquire a pilot's license. He bought a Bonanza to pursue the goal, since a fellow ought to learn to ride the bronco that's in his stable. Bill probably asked if he could mount steer horns over the windscreen.

I'm sure that Bill learned to fly as quickly as his aggressive, successful and confident nature pursued any goal. Bill is an exceptionally intelligent man. He soloed, completed a short solo cross-country, and had his certificate endorsed by his instructor for both adventures.

Let's understand the goal and hence, the budding scenario. He wanted only to fly from office to office. He never intended to carry anyone with him. As Bill interpreted the Federal Air Regulations he was now qualified and legal to do both: Fly solo on cross-country jaunts. He did just that, month after month.

One day the Chief of the local Flight Standards District Office called. "Bill, we often need to get inspectors down to 'Cowtown' and I've noticed you go there a lot. Any chance our fellows could ride with you on occasion?" Why, shucky durn, partner!

Ain't nothing make ol' Bill happier than to help his friends in the FAA! "You send those airborne cowhands right on down to my stall anytime you want."

Student pilot Bill is now illegally carrying passengers and the worst kind: the FAA.

I don't recall exactly how long this persisted, but long enough to renew his medical and get re-endorsed to continue with the activity. In fact, being a bona fide 'good ol boy,' Bill would call the FAA FSDO office when he was a-heading down to 'Cowtown' to see if he could provide transportation.

Bill often traded 'legs' with the Feds. He'd let one of them fly down and Bill would fly back. It was just the best of the aviation world's symbiotics, a general aviation pilot promoting the interests of the FAA and the Feds even giving some dual instruction to an eager student (literally) like Bill.

Finally, in one fell swoop (or 'one swell foop,' however the case may be), Bill received a phone call and summons to visit the FAA FSDO Chief.

As Bill entered, the conversation went like this:

"Bill, I need to see your Private Pilot's license."

"Well, shucks, why for would you need to do that?"

"Bill, please put the license on my desk and let's not debate it."

Bill considered all of his options: social, legal, evasion and available retorts. He finally just stated: "Ah kinda feel like the cowboy who found his first piece of barbed wire." He studied that thing and said, "I don't know what this means, but I think it's the end of the open range."

The only thing better than this story is to hear Bill tell it. It's difficult to be an FAR Advocate and disciplined flight instructor when you're rolling on the floor convulsed with laughter.

In a long career, I've known about and condemned the acts of student pilots carrying passengers. I've even known about an FAR Part 135 Air Taxi operation, owned and operated by a student pilot, transporting remains for funeral homes. (Was he actually 'carrying passengers'? If not, he was still 'flying for hire,' compensation.) But, by golly durn (as Bill might say) when a cowboy is good enough to mount a Bonanza out on the Ponderosa and ride with the Cherokees and Commanches, he needs a witness to that skill. And you can't summon a better witness (or two) to

your hoss-handling skills than the FAA themselves!
Shucks, get a sheriff as a witness, an honest man!

It's lost to my memory what penalty was inflicted upon Bill, but he did return to the skies as a licensed pilot.

Sometime later the electrical system failed in his Bonanza. He was unable to extend the gear. He was self-insured on the hull and would have no property liability in the matter. Bill coordinated the removal of the plane from the runway via UNICOM before he ever landed it.

Bill also owned a big, beautiful Rolls Royce, complete with a driver that particular day. He, too, was advised by UNICOM to drive out to the plane and pick up the Boss. (Small airport, no problem.)

The Bonanza touched down in a bunch of belly-sparks and slid to a stop. Bill exited upon the wing, put on his cowboy hat and gorgeous jacket, faced the tower and executed a magnificent stage-bow, hat in hand extended, bent at the waist. He entered the car and left.

You can never say "hats off" to an illegal operation, carrying passengers on a solo certificate. I can't applaud it. But some of us have been fathers when the misbehavior of one of your own was so amusing that you just laughed too hard to inflict discipline. Bill was no boy; he was a big, lovable, fun and grown-up pixie whose ability to tell the story was exceeded only by his playfulness to create the incident.

Ah, Bill. You still hold a warm sector in my chest of favorite memories and people.

THE GREAT AVIATION QUOTES

The natural function of the wing is to soar upwards and carry that which is heavy up to the place where dwells the race of gods. More than any other thing that pertains to the body, it partakes of the nature of the divine.
—Plato

When once you've tasted flight, you will forever walk the earth with your eyes turned skyward, for there you have been and there you will always long to return.
—Leonardo DaVinci

In order to invent the airplane you must have had at least a thousand years' experience dreaming of angels.
—Arnold Rockman

The most beautiful dream that has haunted the heart of man since Icarus is today reality.
—Louis Bleriot

I fly because it releases my mind from the tyranny of petty things.
—Antoine de Saint-Exupery

To invent an airplane is nothing. To build one is something. To fly is everything.

—Otto Lilienthal

If you are looking for perfect safety, you will do well to sit on a fence and watch the birds; but, if you really wish to learn, you must mount the machine and become acquainted with its tricks by trial.

—Wilbur Wright, 1901

Insisting on perfect safety is for people who don't have the balls to live in the real world.

—Mary Shafer, NASA Ames Dryden

Of the major incentives to provide safety, by far the most compelling is that of economics. The moral incentive, which is most evident following an accident, is more intense, but is relatively short-lived.

—Jerome Lederer

The cause of most aviation accidents: Usually it is because someone does too much, too soon, followed very quickly by too little, too late.

—Steve Wilson, NTSB

Mix ignorance with arrogance at low altitude and the results are almost guaranteed to be spectacular.

—Bruce Landsberg, Executive Director, AOPA Air Safety Foundation

---

[Airplanes are] near perfect, all they lack is the ability to forgive.
—Richard Collins

===

I didn't start this business to make a pile of money. I did it to preserve myself for old age.
—Captain E. B. Jeppesen

===

There is no excuse for an airplane unless it will fly fast!
—Roscoe Turner

===

A 10 cent fuse will protect itself by destroying the $2000 radio to which it is attached.

and

The length of debate about a flight maneuver is always inversely proportional to the complexity of the maneuver. Thus, if the slight maneuver is simple enough, debate approaches infinity.
—Robert Livingston in *Flying the Aeronca*

===

A ship in harbor is safe—but that is not what ships are for.
—John A Shedd

===

[Flying] is the most exciting thing you have ever done with your pants on!
—Stephen Coonts

===

Flying is like sex—I've never had all I wanted, but occasionally I've had all I could stand.

—Stephen Coonts in *Cannibal Queen*

Air racing may not be better than your wedding night, but it's better than the second night.

—Mickey Rupp

Flying is a lot like playing a musical instrument; you're doing so many things and thinking of so many other things, all at the same time. It becomes a spiritual experience. Something wonderful happens in the pit of your stomach.

—Dusty McTavish

A good Captain and good copilot go hand-in-hand. That is, except through the terminal building.

—Len Morgan

The strength of the turbulence is directly proportional to the temperature of your coffee.

—Gunter's Second Law of Air Travel

The three worst things to hear in the cockpit:
The second officer says, "Damn it!"
The first officer says, "I have an idea!"
The captain say, "Hey, watch this!"

—Anonymous

Arguing with a pilot is like wrestling with a pig in the mud; after a while you begin to think the pig likes it.

—Seen on a General Dynamics bulletin board

≡━━≡

"In the Alaska bush I'd rather have a two-hour bladder and three hours of gas than vice versa.

—Kurt Wien

≡━━≡

Lady, you want me to answer you if this old airplane is safe to fly? Just how in the world do you think it got to be this old?

—Anonymous

≡━━≡

"Both optimists and pessimists contribute to the society. The optimist invents the aeroplane, the pessimist the parachute."

—George Bernard Shaw

≡━━≡

"The scientific theory I like best is that the rings of Saturn are composed entirely of lost airline luggage."

—Mark Russell

≡━━≡

When asked why he was referred to as "Ace":
"Because during World War Two, I was responsible for the destruction of six aircraft. Fortunately, three were enemy."

—Captain Ray Lancaster, USAAF

≡━━≡

If helicopters are so safe, how come there are no vintage/classic helicopter fly-ins?

—Anonymous

===

Death is just Nature's way of telling you to watch your airspeed.

—Anonymous

===

Eagles may soar, but weasels never get sucked into jet air intakes.

—Anonymous

===

"I never liked riding in helicopters because there's a fair probability that the bottom part will get going around as fast as the top part."

—Lt. Col. John Wittenborn, USAFR

===

"When it comes to testing new aircraft or determining maximum performance, pilots like to talk about 'pushing the envelope.' They're talking about a two-dimensional model: the bottom is zero altitude, the ground; the left is zero speed; the top is max altitude; and the right, maximum velocity, of course. So, the pilots are pushing that upper-right-hand corner of the envelope. What everybody tries not to dwell on is that that's where the postage gets canceled, too."

—Admiral Rick Hunter, U.S. Navy.

===

"It only takes five years to go from rumor to standard operating procedure."
—Dick Markgraf

===

"Real planes use only a single stick to fly. This is why bulldozers and helicopters—in that order— need two."
—Paul Slattery

===

"I've flown every seat on this airplane. Can someone tell me why the other two are always occupied by idiots?"
—Don Taylor

===

The only real objective of a checkride is to complete it and get the examiner out of the airplane.

===

It is solely the pilot's responsibility to never let any other thing touch his aircraft.

===

If you are not lost you don't care where you are going.

===

I could never be an airline pilot. When they asked what is the most important gauge in the cockpit I always said, "Rounds remaining."

===

When you find yourself straight down doing 500 knots at 500 feet, relax. Otherwise you will just die all tensed up.

===

Speed is life. Until you hit something. Then you die .003 seconds sooner then the guy in back.

〓〓〓

About night flying:
1. The airplane doesn't know it's dark.
2. There are certain aircraft sounds that can only be heard at night. They double in volume over water at night.
3. If you're going to fly at night, it may as well be in weather so you can double your exposure to both hazards.

〓〓〓

One of the most important skills that a pilot must develop is the ability to ignore those things that were designed by non-pilots to get the pilot's attention.

〓〓〓

Selling the airline's airplanes to save money is like stopping the clock to save time.
—Unknown

〓〓〓

The radio can be often dismissed as a suggestion box. The only way to fix it is to turn it off.

〓〓〓

The aircraft load and G-limits are only there if there is another flight intended in that particular airplane. If subsequent flights are not anticipated, such limits do not apply.

〓〓〓

One of the beautiful things about the single piloted airplane is the superb quality of the social experience.

THE MAINTENANCE LOGBOOK

There have been amusing write-ups in airline maintenance logbooks. One of the most memorable was an obviously distracted first officer who wrote, "The autopilot doesn't..." The maintenance technician signed it off as, "It does now."

═══

Another was, "Airplane flies left wing heavy." The A&P mechanic corrected the problem with, "Zeroed out the trim." The next write up was, "Airplane flies with both wings heavy." (That'll fix 'em.)

═══

The following have been passed down through the years:

PROBLEM: Suspected crack in windshield.
SOLUTION: Suspect you're right.

PROBLEM: Radar hums.
SOLUTION: Programmed radar with lyrics.

PROBLEM: Mouse in cockpit.
SOLUTION: Cat installed.

PROBLEM: Noise behind left panels. Sounds like a little man with a hammer.
SOLUTION: Took hammer from little man.

PROBLEM: Whining sound heard on engine shutdown.
SOLUTION: Pilot removed from aircraft.

PROBLEM: Captain's clock is inoperative.
SOLUTION: Wound clock.

PROBLEM: Autopilot tends to drop a wing when fuel imbalance reaches 3000 pounds laterally.
SOLUTION: Flight manual limits permits only 2000 pounds lateral imbalance.

PROBLEM: #2 ADF needle runs wild.
SOLUTION: Caught and tamed #2 ADF needle.

PROBLEM: Left inside tire almost needs replacement.
SOLUTION: Almost replaced left inside tire.

PROBLEM: Test flight OK, except autoland is very rough.
SOLUTION: Autoland not installed on this aircraft.

PROBLEM: #2 engine seeping oil.
SOLUTION: #2 engine oil seepage is normal.
PROBLEM: #1 engine is lacking normal oil seepage.

PROBLEM: Something loose in the cockpit.
SOLUTION: Something tightened in the cockpit.

PROBLEM: Evidence of hydraulic leak on right main gear.
SOLUTION: Evidence removed.

PROBLEM: DME volume unbelievable high.
SOLUTION: Volume set to more believable level.

PROBLEM: Dead bugs on windshield.
SOUTION: Live bugs on back order.

PROBLEM: Autopilot in Altitude Hold varies ± 200 feet.
SOLUTION: Cannot duplicate problem on ground.

PROBLEM: Friction locks cause throttles to stick.
SOLUTION: That's what they are for.

PROBLEM: Number 3 engine missing.
SOLUTION: Engine found on right wing after brief search.

And the SOLUTION that caused every airline pilot to grit teeth:
GROUND CHECKS NORMAL.

The average pilot, despite the swaggering exterior, is fully capable of feeling love, empathy, intimacy, admiration and generosity.

These feelings:
Just don't involve anyone else.

THAT PUP WAS MY COPILOT

On most airline jet aircraft, the forward cargo compartment is heated. That, therefore, is where we can carry live animals. If the heater fails, the Minimum Equipment List stipulates that no live animals may be loaded.

We were the last flight that night from St. Louis to Houston. I'd noted that we have no forward cargo bin heater and the rules precluded carrying live animals that night in that compartment.

The ramp agent arrived in the cockpit to tell me about a dog in a kennel. "Well, I'm sorry," I commented, "but, as you know, we can't load him." The baggage handler felt compassion for the pup, and asked if I'd come down and look at the kennel and situation.

On that dark ramp, I was seeing about one-third of that kennel. It looked small to me. I said, "Oh, heck. Bring it up to the boarding door and let's see what we can negotiate with the flight attendants."

It contained a full-grown Spaniel, about 65 pounds. The flight attendants immediately stated, "No way! You can't put him in the galley. We have no room anywhere for that kennel. No way!" I asked the agent to see if the kennel would even fit in the cockpit, on the floor, behind the pilots. It wouldn't even fit through the door.

While we examined the possibilities, a bespeckled, gentle-looking man, with evident sadness in his eyes came up front and asked, "Am I going to have to stay in St. Louis? That's my dog."

I said: "Well, I hope not. We're trying to figure something out."

He added: "We were booked on Northwest and they cancelled the flight. They rebooked us on TWA. I'm just coming from my father's funeral. That was his dog. I'm trying to take Babe home to Texas."

I asked, "How old is that dog?"

"About nine years old."

"Is she gentle?"

"Very. The sweetest pup on the planet."

"Okay. I want all of you flight attendants to form a wall so the passengers don't observe this. Take her out of the kennel, put her in the cockpit and latch her to that cargo strap. No one is to come up here or open that door en route. I want every passenger off the airplane before I bring Babe out of here."

Ol' Babe lay down and slept the whole way. Occasionally I reached back to scratch her ears and she licked my hand. She was truly "the sweetest pup on the planet."

In Houston, I took off my belt, looped it around Babe's collar and led her up the jetway. The Station Manager was astounded. "You can't do that! That is illegal!"

"What's illegal?" I asked.

"Carrying a dog in the cockpit!"

"No, now wait a minute," I replied. "I looked in the Flight Operations Policy Manual and it says you cannot, under any circumstances, carry a dog in the cabin in other than a kennel. It says nothing about the cockpit. Besides, that dog was twice as smart as my copilot and I needed her help."

Babe's new Pappy was delighted. I was, too. It's nice to be nice to nice people.

In the crew van, the copilot said, "That was really nice of you. You'd better hope he doesn't write a letter of commendation."

Oh m'Gawd! I never thought of that. And he did write one.

I was informed of his letter by an intercompany complimentary letter from the Chief Pilot. The owner's letter appeared in the Reservation Agent's monthly publication: "Captain Gwinn gave my dog genuine first class service. We are forever grateful." It was reprinted twice elsewhere.

I had a Junior Captain certificate made up for Babe and also sent a set of plastic Captain's wings.

One day I asked the Chief Pilot if he wanted to hear 'the whole story' on the transportation of the dog. "I'm sure I don't want to know," he replied.

Arming Airline Pilots
As published in *Plane and Pilot* Magazine
(2004)

Decades ago the Air Mail pilots carried pistols. They probably fired more rounds at oncoming birds than at anyone who wanted Aunt Mary's letter to her nephew in Dodge City, Kansas. There is nothing funny about the need to arm airline pilots. Born in Kansas, however, where we cultivated Wyatt Earp and Doc Holiday, all of us kids had guns. I have enough scars inflicted by the BB guns of my contemporaries to permit me to comment about gun control, which is, of course, the ability to hit the target at which one aims.

Anytime that Congress, the FAA and our security agencies spend over a year considering a subject, the legislation is bound to create a chuckle. In the past we were all enchanted with FAA security videos: "This is a rifle. This is a pistol. This pistol is an automatic. This one has a cylinder." That kind of advanced firearm training kept us awestruck.

Armed airline pilots will go through psychological profiling, three weeks of training, firing range qualification, carry weapons in a lockbox through a terminal building and holster the pistol onboard the airplane. They are not authorized to fire them in the cabin.

First, I'd bypass all of that by simply wearing an empty holster while carrying an empty lockbox. What's the impression? "That guy is packing." I'd also have a patch made for my shoulder: ".357 Qualified." Surely the Feds will encourage pilots with marksmanship medals like the Army: "Sharpshooter" badge with pistol bar. Will a big medal and big gun someday replace the big watch tradition? (Hint: The John Wayne walk is done by placing one foot directly in front of the other in that macho ramble through the terminal building; the shoulder leads the foot on each step.)

What's the effect on Cockpit Resource Management? The first officer is carrying a weapon and the captain isn't? There's a case for courtesy. Who wants to hear his captain say: "Well, I didn't pass the psychological exam. Did you?" (I'd tell that to the first officer whether it was true or not. If I were a first officer I'd say, "I failed the psych test. Something about hating authority, but I got a gun anyway.")

All of this is to prevent or interrupt a hijacking attempt. I flew with several captains named "Jack." On the airplane you introduced yourself with, "Hi, Captain" or "Hi, Sir." It was not a name that invited informality.

Initial cockpit introductory banter was usually, "Where are you from?" or "Where'd you learn to fly?" Now it's, "What ya packing?" ("Oh, I've got a six-round Cobra and I wrote *Captain* on three shells.")

Which reminds me of the Captain who laid a pistol on the instrument panel and remarked, "I carry this just for first officers who get me lost." The first officer pulled out his pistol and said, "Come to think about it, I'll know we're lost before you do." (In today's environment the captain contemplates, "This guy is such a lousy pilot that I won't give him a landing and the government gave him a gun?")

Can't fire in the cabin. For a Kansan this is anathema. I'd want a hijacker stalking forward from the aft lav as I await him in my High Noon stance at the cockpit door. I didn't practice holstered quick-draws as a kid to betray Gene Autry with anything less than a fair fight. I'd wear my hat, too. Gene got into the most tumultuous fistfights and the hat never left his head. (Super Glue?) I can also imagine snarling, "Ya better like the taste of metal, pilgrim, 'cause I'm gonna make you eat that gun."

Recurrent training is interesting to contemplate. Out to the firing range! "OK, this time you have a trigger failure, one jammed shell and your first officer is unarmed. What are you going to do?" Naturally you'd call for the "Trigger failure, Jammed shell and Useless first officer" checklists. ("And please read them fast!")

The Sky Marshall program made sense. I thought, "Here's a splendid opportunity for retired airline captains. Old enough to have patience and appraise the situation. Systems knowledge to know the vulnerable areas of the airplane. Both gray hair and probably paunchy enough to be unapparent as a threat. Put a couple *old men* back there and you have a genuine camouflaged presence." Nope, the maximum age is 37 for that job. If physical conditioning is the requirement, let's contract the World Wrestling Association.

The announcement was that tens of thousands of pilots volunteered for the gun-carrying program, but 46 will be in the initial training. There's a statistic that should comfort our enemies. Forty-six of one hundred thousand makes the odds attractive. That's like saying "Your chances of having a bomb on board is one in one hundred million. So bring your own bomb; the statistical chance of having TWO bombs on board is an infinite quantity." There's nothing like advertising vulnerability. It's marvelous to advertise that less than one percent of airline pilots are armed in the immediate future.

It was inconvenient enough to wrestle your license and medical certificate out of your wallet for an FAA Inspector in the cockpit. Now you'll need your psychological profile to carry the gun-filled lockbox through security screening. Imagine the ego wounds: "You sure aren't as stable as the last captain who went through here. You still hate your mother?"

One major airline issued and insists upon Tazers (electrical shock weapons) in the cockpit. Isn't that sane? If you can fire only IN the cockpit, there's windows, circuit break panels, instruments, ricocheting bullets and of course, a dispensable first officer of no consequence. It's the flight attendants who need the Tazers and have needed them for a long time. Unruly passenger? Put that chap to sleep for a while. "I thought he was having a heart attack and I was defibrillating him."

Regulations often amuse me. Years ago they stated, "To fly at night you must have an electric landing light on the wing." This was, I suppose, to preclude glow sticks or a flashlights taped on the wing. What kind of light COULD you have other than an electric landing light?

I will never be amused at the need for aircraft safety. There is nothing funny about the threat to our industry. The responsibility of using a weapon is never comical. It's just the politicians, appropriately invited to be hosts on Saturday Night Live, who give me grist for a grin. Other than that, I'm devastated at what has come to be.

Trust your pilot:

CAPTAIN DONNY—THE RETURN OF THE ROGUE

Many years ago Don flew Boeing 707s from the West Coast to the East Coast. He always bid the same trip: San Francisco, a stop at St. Louis, and continuing onto New York. One month the company had a schedule change: San Fran non-stop New York; no more stops in St. Louis.

At about 41,000 feet altitude, nearly 100 miles north of St. Louis, Don used the radio:

"St. Louis Ramp, TWA 414, we're on the ground. What gate do you want us to use?"

Shocked silence: "TWA 414, you are WHERE?!"

"We're on the ground; taxi to what gate?"

"But," sputtering, frustrated, "you're not supposed to be here!"

"Whatcha mean? Been landing here every week. Same flight."

"We had a SCHEDULE CHANGE! You don't stop here anymore."

Don gave this a thoughtful pause: "I wondered why we had all this fuel remaining."

The ground agent is still in silent shock.

"Tell ya what," volunteers Don. "I'll just taxi down and take off again. Don't say anything to anyone, okay?"

Utter silence. Stunned, incredulous ground agents.

"Nah, I don't want to do that to you. Put it in the computer that 414 did a touch-and-go landing at St Louis. We'll just continue with the trip."

A touch-and-go with 150 passengers? Unheard of! An approach, landing, power applied in the rollout and then a takeoff, a training maneuver for light airplanes, now allegedly conducted in a Boeing 707 filled with passengers.

When Don arrived at JFK and blocked into the gate, a battalion of officials boarded the plane: Chief Pilot, Flight Managers, FAA, Passenger Supervisors. "WHAT is this report of a touch-and-go landing in St. Louis?"

Don: "I arrive eleven minutes early, with the proper fuel burn, and YOU think I descended and landed at St. Louis? What's wrong with you people? I haven't the least idea what you're talking about."

Captain Don may have enhanced the income of cardiologists from coast to coast.

Don was, however, one of the 'best sticks,' best pilots on the airline. Few people could handle a 707 equal to Don. As a skilled glider/soaring competitor, his sense of time, altitude, energy management and descent rates were all flawless. In fact, Don liked to pull the throttles to idle and make a 'dead stick' landing in San Francisco, virtually gliding a Boeing 707 (from about 10,000 feet) over the Bay to touchdown. It violated every rule in the book; quiet, obedient copilots and flight engineers (in those days) watched with anxiety. He did it flawlessly every time, touching down right on the numbers. Few noticed that Don always gave himself *an out*. With 50 degrees of flaps on a

Boeing 707, he could easily deplete the excess altitude and airspeed when the maneuver was assuredly successful.

One day a Flight Manager (pilot supervisor) was riding in the cockpit. This is like assuring that the teacher is watching before you hurled a spitball across the classroom. When they reached Don's power-off point, Don eased the throttles back, trimmed the airplane for the proper attitude, assured it was in hands-off glide, then turned and looked at the Flight Manager with great solemnity:

"Let us understand, sir. It is more honorable to land in the Bay than it is to touch those throttles."

Don was given six month's return to the copilot's seat for that adventure. Perhaps the penalty time was lessened by every captain begging that Don be re-promoted, to get him the hell out of their cockpit!

Don carried the best looking and smallest flight bag on the airline. In it he had only a Jeppesen manual, the maps and departure and approach charts for TWA airports. The Flight Operations Manual, however, stipulated several items to be carried on the flight deck. On this day Don was getting a checkride. He flew airplanes flawlessly and never worried about them.

"Captain Don, I'm a bit disturbed by your flight bag. Why don't you carry all the required equipment?"

Don looked at the flight engineer: "Do you have the Flight Handbook for the airplane and a tool kit?" He nodded that he did. Don quizzed the copilot: "Do you have the Flight Operations Policy Manual?" He did.

"I don't understand, sir. What are we missing?"

"I'm not going to argue with you, Don. The next time I see you, you'd better have a flight bag like everyone else. Understood?"

Don bought a magnificent flight bag: BIG, embossed with "Captain Don—San Francisco" on the lid. He carried it for about two weeks before encountering that same flight manager.

"That bag is ostentatious, Don, as I'm sure you intended. But at least you have a flight bag worthy of the job."

"I'm glad you like it," Don replied.

Donny sat down the bag, opened the latches, extracted his original, small bag from it, and walked off.

One of the ALPA agreements with Carl Icahn, to attempt salvage of TWA's future, was that annual recurrent training would be 'no pay–no flight credit.' We spent two days in St. Louis, from wherever we lived, absorbed the hotel costs, volunteered the time and resented it. At about this same time the company issued a strict dress code policy for the training center: coat and tie, no exceptions.

The ground instructor upon entering the room could not miss Captain Don seated in the rear of the class: Golf shirt, Dockers slacks, Topsiders with no socks.

At the class break, the instructor approached our infamous Captain: "Sir, do you know the dress code for training?"

"Yes, I do. I surely do. Thanks for asking."

"But…it's coat and tie, Captain!"

"Ohhhhh…" replied Captain Don. "You mean *for training!* Yes, I agree with that 100 percent. But you see Annual Recurrent Training is charity work now; we volunteer our time. When I volunteer for the Salvation Army they just give me a bell and a corner to staff; they don't tell me how to dress."

The instructor hastily retreated to the office of the Director of Training to report and ask what the heck to do!

"Look, you're dealing with Captain Don. Don't oppose him, you'll only give him other ideas or stimulate his imagination. Leave it alone."

As one copilot told me: Captain Don during his simulator checkrides would be telling a joke on takeoff and they'd cut an engine. He would catch the yaw, rotate on speed, climb out flawlessly in one of our most challenging exercises, and never miss the flow or theme of the joke he was telling. I never saw anyone like Don. Flying to him was simply breathing, too natural to merit concentration.

The last time Don and I were together was in the St. Louis ramp office, shortly before he retired. It was the middle of the Icahn era. Morale was dismal, anger was high, tempers were short; uniform pride was non-existent. We were a dying airline, with all of its resources sucked from it and the lives of families, education of children and retirement plans were all in hazard. The ramp office was a tomb. Don signaled to me from a distant corner.

"You know," he began, arms outstretched, "for thirty

years I heard that I was a discipline problem. I was a trouble-maker. I was a detriment to good morale. I was a poor example. I had no standards. Look around me now! I WAS JUST AHEAD OF MY TIME!"

As I recall all the years of a fun career, Captain Don will always remain my favorite personality, my best memories.

The 747, a Grand Bird

When the Boeing 747 reached the airlines it was the first airplane to have electrically adjusted pilot seats. Airlines are procedure addicted. It was only a matter of time for a creative pilot to devise an emergency procedure for this new feature. (Thanks to my pal, Captain Barry Schiff, for keeping a copy of that prized document.)

EXCERPT FROM THE MAINTENANCE MANUAL: RUNAWAY ELECTRIC SEAT PROCEDURE, PILOTS: BOEING 747

GENERAL:

When working in the B-747 cockpit, pull POWERSEAT circuit breaker on the P6 panel before performing any maintenance on or in the area of the Pilot's Seats to prevent accidentally powering the seat. Since these seats are electrically powered, they move at a fast rate and may catch in an awkward position. If an operating, inflight crew experiences "seat runaway," use the following procedure.

ADJUSTMENT:

INITIAL ACTION: Determine which seat is running away. During the stress of routine operations, it is possible to mistake which seat is out of control.

If the Captain's seat is out of control forward, it may appear that the First Officer's seat is running backwards. This is a form of spatial disorientation and will only last until the Captain is emasculated on the control column. Do NOT engage the autopilot at this time, as a violent pitch up will result. In order to determine which seat is the runaway seat, suggested procedure is to awaken the flight engineer for troubleshooting.

SILENCE AURAL WARNINGS:

With the advent of a runaway seat, crew members describe noises of a low rumbling nature followed by the words: "Good God, my seat is out of control!" followed by a piercing scream of increasing intensity (and especially pitch) in cases of forward runaways. As in all emergencies and in order to comply with standardization, the first officer will silence the aural warning by clamping a hand over the Captain's mouth and advise: "Captain's mouth shut...SHUT!" From this point onward, refer to the checklist located on the underside of the Captain's seat cushion.

JAMMED BALLS:

Should the seat runaway in the forward mode, the ball bearings will interlock and jam the seat when it is four inches from the instrument panel. The seat will then be stuck in the forward position and travel no farther forward. The Captain will advise the crew: "I have jammed balls!" The flight engineer will immediately refer to the CAPT. JAMMED BALLS checklist located in the aft lavatory. It is imperative that the crew check for control column damage at this time. If the control column is broken, the crew will advise Dispatch that the Captain has a broken stick and jammed balls.

CIRCUIT BREAKER PULL (RESPONSE: PULL):

The engineer will at this point pull the appropriate circuit breaker to prevent the seat from running up further in the vertical mode which could cause the bearings to overheat and result in a possible ball burst. This would necessitate the use of the BROKEN BALLS checklist. Since the engineer can rarely find the correct circuit breaker, it is suggested that any circuit breaker be pulled at random so as not to delay the completion of the checklist.

NOTE: The Captain's position will prevent him from cross-checking this step.

FIRE CHECK (RESPONSE: CHECK):

When the seat bearings jam and stop forward seat travel, the electrical motor may short out and start a fire under the captain, resulting in a captain's lower aft body overheat. The engineer will advise the captain of the fire, to which the captain will reply: "Fire, my ass!"

SEAT UP:

Should the seat continue to run away in the vertical mode, the first officer will advise "Seat UP...UP!" to which the captain will reply "Mbjejf^t#vtse*ambid!" Captain's reply will vary with height to which his seat has risen. It is suggested procedure to place a pillow at the captain's head and land at the nearest available airport.

BE CAREFUL OUT THERE !

Spot Landing

TRANSPORTING THE DELICATE

Practice layovers are pauses at intermediate stations with two or three hours of time to consume before continuing the trip. A crew doesn't actually *get* to layover and rest, but just sits idly. For example, a crew might pause in Sioux City, Iowa for three hours with a departure that continues their scheduled segments for the day. Practice layovers are nonproductive and boring; we're usually stranded in a ramp office.

My creative, humor-filled pal, First Officer Dave Godec (now a Captain) and I had one three-hour respite in Lincoln, Nebraska. In the ramp office, I noticed a large roll of bright orange tape, about three inches in width and labeled: HUMAN REMAINS—HANDLE WITH CARE. That was pregnant with possibilities.

In an adjacent storage room I found a box, about twelve inches square, and into which I loaded paper, junk, paper clips, actually anything for weight. A handful of paper towels was liberally soaked in water and placed in the container. Then it was bound with orange "HUMAN REMAINS—HANDLE WITH CARE" labels around the circumference and across the top.

This cargo was given to Victor, our gate agent with the request: "When you come to close the aircraft door, give this to the flight attendant and tell her that it needs to go to St. Louis."

Between that exchange and Victor's arrival at the airplane, he'd found yellow rubber gloves reaching from hands to shoulders. He extended the important shipment to the flight attendant with the remark: "This needs to be given to the cockpit and taken to St. Louis."

She noticed that it seemed to drip-drip-drip. "I'm NOT handling that!" she exclaimed. She appeared a bit ashen. She was soon to disassemble.

Victor entered the airplane, then the cockpit and handed the package to Dave Godec. The flight attendant in the doorway was definitely ashen—bloodless white.

I hastened to get busy in my flight bag, on the floor to my left, and obviously oblivious to this activity.

"Hey!" remarked Dave. "Do you know this is leaking?"

"Yes," replied Victor. "That is why I'm wearing the gloves."

Dave lifted two fingers to his lips, licked the tips and said, "Damn. It's really salty."

The flight attendant's knees began to buckle.

I came up from the flight bag, a bit perturbed: "What's going on?"

"Well," says my pal, "We need to take this to St. Louis."

"Give it to me," I snarled.

"Wait a minute, Captain, let me explain…"

"GIVE ME the box!" which I snapped with a gravelly, harsh voice. Dave did so.

"My God! Do you know this thing is LEAKING?" I muttered.

"Yes sir, that's what I wanted to tell you before you took it."

"I'm not taking this," I said, opening the side window and hurled it down to the ramp.

We took a five minute delay to take the flight attendant into the galley and calm her down! Not only did we explain it was a joke, we had to get the box and prove it.

Arriving in St. Louis, and she was now part of the ploy. She asked, "What do you want to do with it now, Smarty?"

"That's easy," I said. "Put it in the oven and let the next crew find it."

We heard nothing more about the adventure in body care.

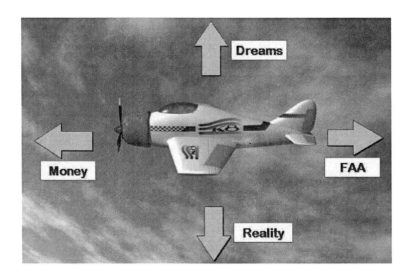

THE CAT AND DUCK METHOD OF INSTRUMENT FLYING

One of my favorites for many years:
Today's flight age is an era highlighted with increasing emphasis on safety. Instrumentation in the cockpit and in traffic control has reached new peaks of electronic perfection to assist the pilot during takeoffs, flight and landing. For whimsical contrast to these and other marvels of scientific flight engineering, it is opportune to remind pilots of the basic rules concerning the Cat and Duck Method of Flight, in case one must revert to basics with failure of sophisticated equipment.

PROCEDURE:
Place a live cat on the cockpit floor. Because a cat always remains upright, the cat can be used in lieu of the turn coordinator, the needle and ball. Merely watch the cat to see which way it's leaning to determine if a wing is low and, if so, which one.

The duck is used for the instrument approach and landing. Because any sensible duck will refuse to fly under instrument conditions, it is only necessary to hurl your duck out of the plane and follow the duck to the ground.,

There are limitations to the Cat and Duck Method, but by rigidly adhering to the following check list, a degree of success will be achieved:

1. Get a wide-awake cat. Most cats do not want to stand upright at all, at any time. It may be necessary to get a large fierce dog in the cockpit to keep the cat's attention.

2. Make sure your cat is clean. Dirty cats will spend all their time washing. Trying to follow a cat licking itself usually results in a tight snap roll, followed by an inverted or flat spin. You can see this is very unsanitary.

3. Old cats are best. Young cats have nine lives, but an old, used-up cat with only one life left has just as much to lose as you do and therefore, will be more dependable.

4. Be wary of cowardly ducks. If the duck discovers that you are using the cat to stay upright—or straight and level—the duck may refuse to leave without the cat. Ducks are no better on instruments than you are.

5. Be sure the duck has good eyesight. Nearsighted ducks sometimes will go flogging off into the nearest hill. Very short-sighted ducks will not realize they have been thrown out and will descend to the ground in a sitting position. The maneuver is quite difficult to follow in an airplane.

6. Use land-loving ducks. It is very discouraging to break out of the clouds and find yourself on final approach for some farm pond in Iowa. Also, the

farmers there suffer from temporary insanity when chasing crows off their corn, and will shoot anything that flies by.

7. Choose your duck carefully. It is easy to confuse ducks with geese because many water fowl look alike. While they are very competent instrument flyers, geese seldom want to go in the same direction as you do. If your duck heads off for the Okefenokee Swamp, you may be sure you have been given the goose.

How to recognize an open cockpit pilot.

WELCOME ABOARD, BY WHOM?

Most flights post a Welcome Aboard sheet, denoting the routes, times, altitudes and names of the crew. The copilot usually prepares that and hands it to the forward flight attendant.

It's nonsense, actually. When the flight attendant announces, "In charge of your flight is Captain David Gwinn, assisted by First Officer Dave Godec," I could always imagine some passenger commenting: "Hey, I know those guys by reputation. They do good work." Does anyone really care who is flying the airplane, given that they trust the airline and FAA to staff it with competence?

In that same vein, how about that announcement: "We'll be landing on Runway 27." Aren't you tempted to turn to your seatmate and say: "That's one of the really smooth ones at this airport. I'm glad to hear it." Who cares! Who cares about the entire route announced over the PA while you're still sitting at the gate? I flew them for thirty years and can't envision the route as fast as pilots are conveying the information now that I'm a passenger. Never made one of those myself.

Anyway…the Welcome Aboard Sheet.

Captain Lynn and I were flying together for an entire month. A fun man! I told him, "When I get on the plane I will introduce myself as Justin. I'll assure she doesn't see my name on my flight bag. When you get on, ask if Justin is there yet. That will further implant the name in her mind."

It did. Not only did she call me Justin for the entire day, but she announced, "In command of your flight is Captain Lynn, assisted by First Officer Justin Credible."

Justin Case was an option. Since we did not have a Flight Engineer on DC-9/MD-80 aircraft, we'd often enter Ben Deleted as that crewmember for that slot on the Welcome Aboard Sheet. They usually caught that one before they announced it.

"THE GUY AHEAD OF YOU ... HAD A SMOOTH RIDE"

Ah, What'd I Say? Who's Offended?

Captain Jerry was one of the pilots who bid to fly for Saudi Arabian Airlines under the TWA monitoring/developmental contract with that country. Many pilots went to Saudi for extended periods of time, enticed by the big money and benefits. In time they returned to TWA-USA.

Jerry was on his first domestic trip since his return: JFK-Las Vegas. We were to enjoy a lengthy layover in the play-city. As the Boeing 707 crossed into Colorado, Jerry remarked: "There is that _____ Power Plant that you've been reading about." He pointed to some object on the ground that I never did see.

"What power plant, Jerry? I don't know anything about a power plant."

(Impatiently) "That one! The _____ Power Plant."

"Never heard of it."

"Well," picking up the PA microphone, he responded, "Everyone else has."

With that, Jerry announced to the passengers:

"Ladies and Gentlemen, passing on the left side of the airplane is the _____ Power Plant that has caused all the trouble out here between the Indians and the white people."

I was mumbling my third "Houston, we have a problem!" when the flight attendant began banging on the door with lots of energy.

"We have a man in first class who is enraged. He wants the Captain back there right now."

"Ummm, what do you suppose that's about?" Jerry mused.

"I think it's about the Indians and the white people, Jer, not a really politically astute comment," I suggested.

"Well," straightening himself in his seat, in command, making a decision, "why don't YOU go on back there and find out what the problem might be."

Two conditions in First Class made this better than it could have been. The complaining passenger was the only occupant of First Class. The curtain was drawn between First Class and Coach. No one was witnessing what was bound to be embarrassing. This gentleman is standing up and poised over the seat in front of him like a panther awaiting prey, ready to pounce. As a predator, however, he was obviously snockered, face flushed and the fumes were intoxicating.

"Hello," I began. "How are you, sir?"

"Are you the Captain?!"

"No, sir, I'm not. The Captain is very busy, but wanted to assure that any problem was promptly addressed. How can I help?"

"I want an apology. I want a public and personal apology. I am *one-eighth Cherokee Indian.* That announcement was an insult."

"Wow!" I spoke with ultimate sympathy, "You're right! Let's sit down for a minute. I really feel badly."

Being as nice a man as an angry one, he agreed to sit and talk. The alcohol fumes were hazardous.

"First let me say that you do deserve an apology. That was a poor choice of words. I hope you can forgive us."

"Well," he softened. "I was really insulted by that."

"Yes," I agreed, "and you should have been. I will see that the Captain apologizes in any format you might accept. By the way, I'm Dave Gwinn." I offered my hand.

"I'm _____," he replied. One of the best-known sports commentators on television. I hadn't recognized him.

"Sir, I think the Captain will gladly apologize to you. Right now he is very busy with the lives of 150 people in his hands. I think that Jerry is going to be very, very upset that he has upset you! He is a kind and considerate person. Would you consider permitting him to apologize when we're on the ground in Las Vegas? I really hate to disturb him, and this will, while he's in command of the airplane."

"Well," he softens more. "I guess that he *cares* is the important thing."

"Absolutely! He is a gentle man. It was a poor choice of words, but he wouldn't hurt you or anyone for anything. Please forgive us."

"Well, okay," the passenger concludes. "Let's just forget it. It seemed pretty crass and insensitive, but we all make mistakes. He doesn't have to apologize."

"You're so very kind, sir. I always suspected you were when I watched you on television."

I summoned the flight attendant: "Please give Mr. _____ anything he wants. We have offended him and let's be extra kind."

This has taken ten minutes to pacify this very good man. We visited a bit more and I said that I really had to return to the cockpit. The crisis was over.

When I entered the cockpit the Captain was about as mad as the victim.

"Where the hell have you been?!"

"Hey, I was back there wiping war paint off of _____. You really offended him with that Indians-white people remark."

"Yeah? Well, to hell with him!"

So much for that kind, caring, sensitive Captain that I assured our celebrity was in charge.

Some of the Best of Aviation Poetry

Because I fly
I laugh more than other men,
I look up and see more than they,
I know how the clouds feel,
What it's like to have the blue in my lap,
To look down on birds,
To feel freedom in a thing called the stick.

Who but I can slice between God's billowed legs,
And feel them laugh and crash with His step?
Who else has seen the unclimbed peaks?
The rainbow's secret?
The real reason birds sing?
Because I fly,
I envy no man on Earth.

    —Anonymous

Courage is the price that Life exacts for granting peace.
The soul that knows it not knows no release from little
  things;
Know not the livid loneliness of fear,
Nor mountain heights where bitter joy can hear
The sound of wings.
How can life grant us boon of living, compensate

For dull gray ugliness and pregnant hate
Unless we dare the Soul's dominion?
Each time we make a choice, we pay
With courage to behold the restless day,
And count it fair.

—Amelia Earhart

An airman is always free, sir
To land with a bump or a greaser.
Any old clunk,
Can land with a thump,
But pros go for smoothie crowd pleasers.

—Anonymous

Come to the edge.
We might fall.
Come to the edge.
It's too high!
COME TO THE EDGE!
And they came,
And he pushed,
And they flew.

—Christopher Logue

An Airman Grace

Lord of thunderhead and sky
Who place in man the will to fly
Who taught his hand speed, skill and grace
To soar beyond man's dwelling place
You shared with him the Eagle's view
The right to soar, as Eagles do
The right to call the clouds his home
And grateful, through your Heavens to roam
May all assembled here tonight
And all who love the thrill of flight
Recall with twofold gratitude
Your gift of Wings, Your gift of Food.

—Father John MacGillivary
Royal Canadian Air Force

AIR TRAFFIC CONTROL

I've had rewarding experiences and acquired the utmost respect for Air Traffic Controllers. When you hear one of these professionals handle a dozen airplanes in the New York terminal area, non-stop directives, never losing "the picture," you know you're observing a superior intellect. But that doesn't mean we don't have fun as well. Never underestimate a controller—they have a hotline to Eddie Murphy and Robin Williams.

Leaving a Midwest point, the controller said, "TWA, say heading."

I replied: "3-8-0."

Without a pause, he directed, "Turn to a heading of 4-1-0 and you're cleared direct to Henderson."

Leaving Columbus, Ohio we encountered birds and two strikes just above the windshield. I've reported many bird strikes, but waited twenty years for the controller to ask something other than "say location and altitude."

Me: "Columbus, we just took two bird strikes on departure."

ATC: "Where did you hit them?"

Me, grinning: "Right in the head, as far as we could tell."

― ▪ ―

Despite their competence, ATC can be frustrated:
"TWA, are you on the frequency?"
"No."
"Er...OK."

― ▪ ―

It was always fun to me to check on an en route frequency with: "Center, TWA 414 is level at 3-5-0 and the last controller promised us that you'd give us direct to (wherever)."

One replied: "Well, he's sitting right next to me. I'll ask him about that."

My reply: "Oh, forget it. He's probably just baiting both of us."

― ▪ ―

It is also helpful when you advise ATC that you are "Radar vector equipped" or "Slam-dunk qualified" to expedite any trip.

― ▪ ―

One TWA Captain told ATC: "We're in one of the 727s equipped with this new GPS. We need to test it direct to L.A. if you can accommodate us and advise us of the accuracy of the equipment." We *never* had GPS!

When ATC told him he was "about 20 degrees off course," the Captain hastened to agree and confirm, "We were waiting for you to acknowledge that. Our equipment indicated that and we'll correct and give it another try."

He got the best routing of the day.

===—===

When you're advised, "Traffic at 6 o'clock," some of the controllers are not amused when you respond, "Is that local or Zulu time?" (With the advent of the digital watches it was amusing to watch youngsters with no ready concept of "a quarter to four" or an o'clock position.)

===—===

There are many fast retorts that I've overheard:
In Atlanta: "Atlanta tower, what are calling your winds?"
Them: "Mariah."

===—===

Or "TWA, how do you read?"
Reply: "About 2000 words a minute if I'm rested."

===—===

One of my favorites was:
"TWA, can you give me a short count?"
Answer: "Yes."
"WILL you give me a short count?"
"Sure. Eenie-meany-miney-moe, moe-miney-meany-eenie."

===—===

Arriving at the outer marker, the airliner transmitted, "Outer-marker inbound for Runway 30-L."
No answer. After three more efforts to communicate, the tower replied, "Stand by. We're changing controllers."
Captain: "What do you use? Pampers or Huggies?"

As a general aviation instructor and clearing the runway, the tower advised, "We're not speaking to that helicopter on the ramp."

I replied; "Okay, I too will not socialize with him."

Overheard in the Midwest:

"(Airline), what are you vacating?" (meaning leaving an altitude, of course).

Reply: "This year the last two weeks of July. How about yourself?"

My all-time favorite was a turbulence report:

"Center, it's so rough up here that the Captain just stabbed himself with his dinner fork."

A chuckling controller asked a Southern-based airline: "How's your ride?"

Reply: "Shucks, I dunno. We haven't eaten yet."

Our flight from JFK to STL was plagued with turbulence. No matter what altitude we requested, it got more uncomfortable. The DC-9s and MD-80s were restricted to the upper 30,000-foot options.

After several altitude efforts, we said, "We'll have to live with it. There's no smooth altitude."

A Lear captain came on the frequency, obviously amused: "It's smooth at flight level 410." (41,000 feet MSL.)

Another high performance corporate aircraft transmitted: "It's smooth at flight level 430, too."

Next we heard: "Yeah? How's the PAY up there?"

≡━━≡

The competition with ATC is one of electromagnetic energy. I acquired one of those multi-sound-duplication boxes at a gimmick store and waited to use it.

ATC: TWA, traffic at 2 o'clock and high.

ME: In sight, locked on and firing.

(rat-tat-tat, boom, whistling missiles)

ATC: Score one kill, TWA. Paint a 737 on the side of your airplane.

≡━━≡

Unknown landing signal officer to carrier pilot after his sixth unsuccessful landing attempt: "You've got to land here son, this is where the food is."

≡━━≡

Instrument flight intersections have names. Sometimes they are geographic, sometimes a tribute to a retired controller, sometimes not readily recognized as any possible identity, unless you're told, like RAZIM in Detroit.

Arriving DTW, I noted we had a new intersection: MIZAR.

Me: "Approach, I know where MIZAR came from, but where did you get RAZIM?"

Approach: "RAZIM is MIZAR spelled backwards."

Me: "Well, I guess if I were lex-dysic, I'd have recognized that."

Silence. I told the copilot: He didn't get it!

Approach: "TWA, contact the tower. Have a nice yad."

═ ═══ ═

In St. Louis, home of Budweiser and Anheuser-Busch, Inc., a major financial entity and employer, it was surprising to see that someone thought COORS would be an appropriate name for an ATC intersection. I gave it about ten days longevity. Right! It got renamed pronto.

═ ═══ ═

Memorable ATC quips:

"If you can hear me, traffic no longer a factor."

"You have to key your mic and speak. I can't hear you when you nod your head."

"Put your compass on E and get out of my airspace."

"If you want more room, Captain, push your seat back."

═ ═══ ═

Some controllers can talk faster than six people can listen. There have to be sonic booms ricocheting in the control room. Airline pilots need to know how to handle that.

Center: "TWAturntoaheadingof240,climbtoFL270, maintain250knotsuntilpassing FL170andcontactKansasCity Centeron132.5."

Huh?

You: "Center, we have a problem here. Stand by."

Center: "State the nature of the problem."

You: "I said stand by. I don't think we have an emergency YET."

Now you address the first officer: "Okay, I'm gonna check back on. You try to get the altitudes and speeds, I'll try to get the headings and frequency."

═━═

There's an alternative to the above, but it doesn't work well in air carrier operations:

You: "Center, this is the instructor. My student didn't get all of that. Can you repeat it to him a bit slower?"

═━═

Remember there is one identity that clears the pattern and acquires all of the attention you'd like: Student pilot. ("Tower, this is TWA. I'm a student pilot and would appreciate your help.")

═━═

After some antagonistic exchanges between the captain and the controller, with some misunderstandings on both sides, the captain inquired:

"Are *you* a Trainee?"

Infuriated, ATC replied, "I certainly am NOT!"

Captain: "Got one we can talk to?"

═━═

Landing at Nashville, one airline quipped to ATC:

"That altimeter setting you gave us has us 15 feet underground."

ATC: "Roger. Up periscope and taxi to the ramp."

═━═

ATC: "Cessna 56 Romeo, give me a rough time check."

56 Romeo: "It's Tuesday, sir."

ATC, after a confusing conversation with a disturbed student pilot:

ATC: "Do you have enough fuel or not?"

Student: "Yes."

ATC: "Yes WHAT?"

Student: "Yes, SIR!"

ATC: "Citation 59 Uniform, turn right to heading 3-5-5 and report your heading."

59U: "Roger. 341-342-343-344-345…"

FSS Briefer: "Threshold of Runway 18 is displaced 277 feet."

Student: "Is that MSL or AGL?"

On after-midnight flights from LA to STL, you might hear, "Cleared direct to St. Louis. Take up a 090 degree heading." Then it's a long boring flight with no activity except switching frequencies every twenty or thirty minutes. Utterly exhausting with no activity. However, I did discover from that altitude on a dark night how *many* airports you can find by clicking your microphone seven times on a Unicom frequency. Those runways leap in illumination from complete darkness. I called it "Find the airports." I always imagined some ol' boy living at the airport nudging his wife and saying, "Come on, we gotta get up. Some airplane is landing."

===---===

I used one of the headsets with attached microphones once…and once only. In fact, my intent was to enhance the long, all-night flight by conveying *all* of the really great jokes I knew. They were plentiful and not for mixed company. After a couple of hours and no frequency change instructions, we discovered my mic switch was stuck in the transmit position. I like to think of it as being an airborne Redd Foxx.

===---===

A lost student pilot pleading for help is not that unusual. One was told to circle the water tower around the town he reported in front of him and "tell me the name of it."
Student: "It says Seniors '98."
Another was asked: "What was your last known position?"
Student: "When I was Number 1 for takeoff."

===---===

There are few talents to match the delivery and storytelling of Rod Machado. He's simply brilliant. And this is one of my favorites among the stories he tells:
After an airshow at a nearby airport, a Cessna 150 awaited takeoff. A C-5 Air Force cargo plane taxied behind him. Now that critter is huge—the second biggest plane in the world, dwarfing this tiny Cessna.

The C-5 crew realized they'd left a jeep behind. They inquired whether they had to taxi back or could the jeep be delivered to them in their present position? The jeep was cleared to approach the C-5.

Now if you've ever seen a C-5 take on cargo, the entire nose section lifts upward...like a great big mouth. And a ramp slides out like a big hungry tongue! The Cessna 150 pilot heard the noise and perceived the movement behind him and looked rearward at that airborne cannibal.

"Tower, what's going on behind me?"

A C-5 pilot picked up the mic and said, "We're gonna eat ya', little buddy."

After a pause the tower added: "Yeah, it sure looks like he's gonna eat ya', little buddy."

━━━━

A similar story is about the Cessna 150 and Boeing 707 facing one another awaiting takeoff. ATC asked, "Who is number one down there?"

The Cessna instructor transmitted, "Aw....just let our little buddy go first." The Cessna was cleared for takeoff and surely chuckling.

The tower then asked, "Big Boeing, you're cleared for takeoff, say requested heading."

Answer: "Aw, we'll just follow our little buddy until we can fly over him."

(For non-pilots, the wing-tip vortices, called propwash in the old days, is violent beneath and behind a big airplane. Most certainly the chuckling stopped in the Cessna. It's called a "pirouetting head" in the business.)

━━━━

Nothing was more of pride to TWA than the on-time arrival statistics, number one in the industry. Despite many pleas for a concession that pilots deserved and was of no cost to the company, we were ignored. The TWA pilots went every possible path for recognition of the problem and mutual resolution. Nothing happened. Someone neglected to consider that WE made that on-time arrival happen...or not happen.

One day was declared NOT-on-time arrival day, more than 15 minutes late. It not only succeeded to a 65% participation level, but ATC assisted me. We were the last flight to Toronto. Once our DC-9 was handed off to the Center, we were instructed:

"TWA, maintain FL230 and 270 knots." (That's about 12,000 feet too *low* and 100+ knots too *slow*.)

"Roger."

From St. Louis to Cleveland, that's where we flew. The copilot asked if he should mention the restriction to Center?

"No. They know what they're doing. Let it be."

Finally we heard from Center: "TWA, we thought you were a prop-driven Trans-World Express flight! Wow, we've kept you far too low. What altitude do you want?"

Me: "Oh, I guess this is fine. We're close now."

Needless to say we had a convulsing TWA President on the phone the next day—and a bit more attention to the problem.

＝＝＝

One pilot probably created every possible situation in his mind to have a retort for Air Traffic Control. His flight #553 was repeatedly misidentified by the controller:

"Airliner 353, contact Cleveland Center on 135.6."

(No answer.)

"Airliner 353, contact Cleveland Center on 135.6."

(No answer.)

"Airliner 353, you're like my wife. You never listen."

Captain: "Center, this is 553, maybe if you called her by the right name she'd be more attentive.

===

As an aside, my wife and I have only ever had one conflict. She says I don't listen to her. I'm not sure, I *think* that's what she said.

Having taught radar for two decades and explaining frequencies, I volunteer a rationalization to you. "My dear, I flew as an instructor for many years, in piston airplanes, long before we attended to ear protection. Therefore, with all the engine noise over a few thousand hours aloft, I have some ear damage. You see, low frequency voices like a man's are very penetrating and carry. High frequency voices, like a lady's, do not. So I have difficult distinguishing what you've said or that you said anything." (Didn't work for me, but it's worth a try in your house.)

===

Tower: "Eastern 702, contact Departure on 124.7."

Eastern: "Roger. By the way we saw some kind of dead animal on the runway during the takeoff roll."

Tower: "Continental 635, cleared for takeoff. Did you copy that report from Eastern?

Continental: "Cleared for takeoff. Roger. Yes, we copied Eastern and we've already notified our catering service."

———

O'Hare: "United 329 Heavy, your traffic is a Fokker, one o'clock, three miles and eastbound. Report contact."

United: "Approach, I've always wanted to say this...I've got that Fokker in sight."

———

Awaiting clearance on the ground in Munich, an American crew overheard this exchange:

Lufthansa (in German): "Ground, what is our clearance time?"

Ground (in English): "If you want an answer, speak English, the international aviation language."

Lufthansa: "I am a German, flying a German airplane in German airspace. Why must I speak English?"

Unknown (but British): "Because you lost the bloody war, that's why!"

———

The student on a night flight and euphoric with his achievement decided to have fun with the tower. On initial contact he transmitted: "Guess who?"

The controller shut off all the lights on the airport and replied: "Guess where?"

———

To a captain demanding priority handling for his own convenience, the female controller stated, "The last time I gave a pilot everything he wanted I was on antibiotics for two weeks."

Equally good retort:
Female controller to airline flight: "Can I turn you on at 7 miles?"
Captain: "Ma'am, you're welcome to try and I'm complimented."

One airline advertised itself as "The World's Most Experienced Airline." One ground controller inquired, "Where is the world's most experienced airline going today, without a clearance?"

I believe it was in one of Robert Serling's superb books: At Washington National on a high-volume day, planes were stacked well into the skies awaiting sequence and landing. Finally one exasperated statement came over the frequency, "This is bullshit."

The controller snapped, "Who said that?"

After a pause, the litany began:

"Continental 414, negative on the bullshit."

"TWA 532, negative on the bullshit."

"Eastern 122, negative on the bullshit."

Soon a controller, choking with laughter, said, "OK, guys, knock it off. I asked for it and we'll forget it."

PRIVATIZED ATC?

AS PUBLISHED IN *PLANE & PILOT* MAGAZINE

In 1981 with the "Shootout at the PATCO Corral," President Ronald Reagan mounted up and shot 10,000 ATC controllers out of the saddle—fired with their effort to strike. We had a couple of months of Agonizing Traffic Chaos, but the system functioned. Hiring and training new controllers was conducted at a frantic pace. Things seemed to return to normal, other than our overall sadness that 10,000 qualified professionals were unemployed. The issues, right or wrong, are not mine to discuss or evaluate.

Thus began the possibilities and discussions of privatizing ATC, outsourcing domestically in the private sector under contracts. Thanks to Phil Boyer and AOPA, my pal Tom Haines (*AOPA Pilot* Editor) tells me that creative thinking has been defeated. Nonetheless, my fertile mind of amusement has to consider all the aspects of that concept.

I spoke with a splendid gentleman at COPA (Canadian Owners and Pilots Association) about their privatized non-profit system. Pilots are billed $65 Canadian per quarter (to be elevated to $72 in the near future). Non-profit is simply not the American way.

While I'm not opposed to paying my own way, as proven by painful bloodletting every April 15th, surely we should be discussing all of the privatized options before implementing any such system. Profit is the core of capitalism and must always be factored into the implementation. This means also, pilots will have to economize.

In example, can't one simply subscribe to a sector like the Southeast and not venture beyond it? Or better yet, pay for one takeoff and one landing with a filed flight plan? I suppose a diversion for weather or an emergency to a non-specified airport would carry a premium, in lieu of total sector coverage.

Consider Dallas, with five basically general aviation airports surrounding it. Would we be seeing TV advertising inducing us to use one, rather than a competitor? Might there be punch cards—five landings and one free? How would this work with students doing touch-and-goes: $100 for the lesson and $200 in airport usage cost? Might you get a non-ATIS discount? "I promise not to use ATIS and assume full responsibility for the operation." Think about ATC Gift Certificates!

There's no way we'd privatize without postings in the stock market: ATCP (Air Traffic Control Profit). If they want to privatize Social Security, ATC might be a good investment. Then, however, we'd get a robber baron (as we've experienced two within the airlines). They'd buy a controlling interest, begin selling off towers, radio equipment and even beacons. We'd get clearances by signal flags or cell phone.

What if your subscription expired on final approach? Would you be compelled to give a credit card number over the frequency? Maybe we'd have a swipe device in the cockpit for a debit card. No doubt you'd hear those dreaded words: "After landing, contact the tower."

In Canada the airlines pay for mileage in the system. There's a case for "Unable!" when given a vector or holding pattern. You can only tie, never successfully compete for the low-level flight award, but surely there'd be a way to get under the radar tracking, just appear at the airport and announce that you are returning, not arriving. Maybe if everyone filed as "Air Canada flight number XXX," the rate would be less expensive than being a foreign American carrier.

It's anticipated that 11,000 or 73% of today's ATC personnel will reach retirement age by 2014. (Interestingly, I recall reading the Social Security funds might face a crisis in that same year!) ATC is funded by the Aviation Trust Fund, in which 7.5% of passenger fares are diverted to it. With airline competition and cheaper fares, that funding has fallen 8% in the last four years. It's definitely time to sell towers, beacons, radio equipment and conduct air traffic from personal vans and CB radios. "Roger, good buddy, pedal to the metal at 170 knots and we be cleared to smack that cement. That's a big 10-4. Refuel and talk to you on the flip side." A flight of two is obviously a convoy and a 747 is an 18-wheeler.

There will be job creations, as promised by the President. The FAA will hire 12,500 new Air Traffic Controllers over the next decade. That reminds me of once asking an ill-tempered controller: "Are you a trainee?" He snapped with hostility that he was not! "Have you got one I can talk to?" My receiver began to smoke. Avionics operate with smoke. You keep the smoke IN the box. Have you ever seen any avionic device smoking and then operate afterwards? Of course not: Keep the smoke IN the box.

Controllers are eligible to retire at age 56. The FAA will seek an exemption permitting them to work until age 61. Airline pilots have mandatory retirement at age 60, due to our obvious deterioration of cognitive skills and health. In the latter case it's high blood pressure, trying to get a word in edgewise or acknowledge a clearance at JFK, DFW or ORD.

Beyond privatizing, there's outsourcing. When I call AOL Technical Support, I'm talking to a heavily accented 'Steve' in India. With satellite technology it might be tempting to outsource ATC to India. What the heck, we've got a few American controllers whom I can't understand with their Mach 2 delivery. Whether those folks can handle both AOL and ATC simultaneously has yet to be disproved. If they are unable, you might be asked for your Screen Name and Password.

Well, it hasn't happened and AOPA has moved aggressively to assure it won't. As Tom Haines stated, "We have the best, most efficient and flexible ATC system in the world. It's not broke. It needs fine-tuning on occasion, but not fixing." I'm indifferent. I've gotten to visit with Steve in India so often that I can understand every fifth word. Some times that's more clarity than I've had at major airports.

Incidentally, the last I read on the national debt, our per capita share was $435,000. It was painful to write a check for that, but I had to put my wife's share on a Visa credit card. Pay now. It can only get more expensive.

Hurricane Wilma

ATIS: Automatic Terminal Information Service

Many thanks to Bill Turcotte, DO, for compiling the best answers to an ATIS inquiry.

A TIS is a frequency wherein the airport conditions are broadcast. The active runway, winds, altimeter, cloud cover and visibility is given to the pilots. This relieves the controllers from repeating the same information over and over. One acknowledges receipt of the information by "I have _____," whatever the phonetic alphabet letter designates the most recent recording (i.e., Alpha, Bravo, Charlie, etc.)

===

Many great replies have been given by pilots when queried whether they had that information:

Do you have Charlie?

"Negative. We left him at the hangar."

Do you have Echo?

"Negative. We're receiving you loud and clear."

Do you have Hotel?

"Negative. We're staying with friends."

Do you have Juliet?

"Negative, and please don't mention her to my wife."

Do you have Kilo?

"Negative, but there's a couple of roaches in the ashtray."

Do you have Mike?

"Negative. I have a push-to-talk headset."

Do you have Oscar?

"Negative, but I'm expecting a nomination this year?"

Do you have Papa?

"Negative, but I did write him this week."

Do you have Uniform?

"Negative, just jeans and a sports shirt."

Do you have Victor?

"Negative. Who is Victor?"

Do you have X-Ray?

"Negative. Just a CAT scan recently."

Do you have Whiskey?

"Negative, not in the last eight hours. Am I off my heading?"

MY MILITARY CAREER

These are non-flying stories, but just too splendid not to share with you. It was in the Army that I saw a Mohawk observation plane land for our inspection and decided: This will be my future. I wanted to fly airplanes. Actually as a boy I saw "The High and The Mighty" with John Wayne. That night in bed I dreamed of becoming a pilot. The military exhibition rekindled that enthusiasm.

═══

After growing up in a military school (Missouri Military Academy) from age twelve to high school graduation, going into the Army was like military school with fewer rules. I'd had a severe knee injury at MMA and was assured I was 4-F, ineligible for the draft. When I got drafted they couldn't seem to find a flaw in my body. I was now a Private (E-1) in boot camp at Fort Leonard Wood, mid-winter, temperatures mostly below zero. That's where I discovered 'cold can be painful.' Later, upon reaching Fort Gordon, Georgia, and for two hours after arrival, I realized that I actually had feeling in my feet!

═══

We were the first Basic Training unit issued the new M-16 combat rifle. Security was intense in accounting for those weapons. Whenever I overheard some Sergeant mention PT (physical training) after the evening meal, I'd switch rifles from one barracks to another. One mention that everyone had better check their rifle numbers resulted in someone running to the Orderly Room to report he had the wrong rifle. So we stood at attention in our warm barracks while they accounted for all the weapons and reprimanded these incompetent misfits. You have to know the rules to know how to break them without penalty.

———

At Fort Gordon, I became a Cryptographer, coding and decoding security messages (Top Secret-Crypto clearance). Despite the fact that my friends and I elevated Budweiser stock to record values all through our training, my grades put me in competition for the White House Communications Center. (I didn't get the job, but the delay in the decision precluded me from joining my classmates, who were equally split between Korea and Viet Nam).

———

I was a "Hold Over" during this decision time: not a student, not assigned on orders. The first morning the Master Sergeant yelled, "Students in one platoon, Hold Overs in a second." Back in those days it seemed enlisted promotions were by tenure only. The incompetents were assigned to training companies to not disrupt the entire Army. That Master Sergeant headed my list as one of the most dense, mentally deficient gentlemen I'd ever met. Nice guy, just not too alert. He was nothing akin to the professional soldier in today's Army.

Once the Hold Over platoon was assembled, the Sergeant walked each line and mumbled: "OK, I have Brown, Smith, Gwinn..." writing our names on his clipboard. We loaded foot lockers all morning. After noon mess, he walked the line and said. "Okay, I have Brown, Smith, Krieger, Gwinn..." Wait a minute, I thought. There's a BIG difference between who is here and who is supposed to be here. If being 'here' is the qualification, watch my action!

The next morning I watched the formation from the barracks with an untied boot. If my absence was noted I intended to stumble out of the barracks, apologizing, embarrassed and reporting for duty. I was never missed. Nor did I ever again report for any after-mess formation for three weeks.

===

In sandy Georgia someone decided, in the absence of grass, to outline the company area in white-washed telephone poles. The Hold Overs were cutting, painting and planting. I usually watched from the barracks for awhile and then left for the PX, library or any other enjoyable consumption of the day.

It was dangerous to be in the company area! This mission must defy detection. I did, however, one day linger too long. I saw the Sergeant about 45 seconds before he saw me. There was a 3 foot piece of telephone pole on the ground which I immediately hoisted to my shoulder. Walking by the Sergeant I yelled, "Good morning, SIR!" (One does not address non-commissioned officers as 'sir.' Obviously I am a young innocent.)

"Hey, you!" yelled this General Patton wanna-be.

"Yes, sir?" was my timid reply.

"What are you doing?!"

I looked up at the pole, then at him: "What am I doing? I'm carrying this telephone pole to another site, sir!"

"Well, then…er, Gwinn…get the lead out and get moving!"

"YES, SIR"…and I trotted off as fast as possible, suppressing my hilarity.

The entire philosophy of the 1960s Army dawned on me that day: If someone was doing something, someone told them to do it (else they'd not be doing anything). Therefore, you do not interrupt an assignment given. I put that telephone pole in the furnace room, and wherever I went for the next two weeks, I carried it. Sometimes I carried it staggering in returning from PX refreshments, but I carried it.

Upon leaving Fort Gordon, I willed that telephone pole to another Private and educated him in Army philosophy. For all I know it's still being carried at Fort Gordon.

Few of those Sergeants would make it in today's Army: demanding physical fitness tests, rigidly observed promotion potential, and out of the Army in the absence of either.

═ ■ ■ ═

My next assignment was Fort Benning. Somehow my administrative talents were recognized and I was a Private First Class assigned to the Commanding General, writing his letters, reviewing files, etc. Plush job and I lived off-post.

This was during the time that racial riots were ripping Selma, Alabama, and our 2d Infantry Division was supplying troops to contain it.

The phone rang: "Office of the Commanding General, Captain Dixon, sir," spoke the commissioned aide.

"Captain Dixon, this is President Kennedy. May I please speak to General Billingslea?"

"YES, SIR!" Dixon fell over his chair and nearly tore the General's door from the frame to announce the Commander in Chief was on the line.

"Okay, son. Just relax." The General took the call.

One more call: "Office of the Commanding General, Captain Dixon, sir."

"Dixon, this is the Attorney General. Get me Billingslea and get him now."

"Well, I'd do that, sir," replied Dixon, "except he is talking to the President."

Minor pause: "Well, okay. I'll wait then, if it's all right."

How I chided Captain Dixon! "You didn't have the guts to say, 'He's talking to your big brother'!"

I always reported directly to the General's office for work. I'd advised them in the company area that "If you need me, call the General's office." NO ONE calls the General's office unless it can't be avoided. I was a virtual unknown in Headquarters Company.

One day, however, I did visit the company area, read the bulletin board and discovered that not only was I assigned KP (Kitchen Patrol) but it was TODAY. KPs reported at about 4 a.m. It's now noon and I've heard nothing about it. This is bad. It required visiting the mess hall to see if I was recognized, missed and in trouble. To do so meant taking off my blouse with my name thereon to preclude assisting recognition. I walked in wearing only a white T-shirt.

In the back was a raging African-American soldier, scrubbing greasy pans and mouthing about every expletive created. "I had KP two weeks ago. This is *&^%@# ridiculous." I noticed his name: GWYNN.

Yes, my conscience bothered me. Then again, if you want the prestige of a good Irish-Welsh name like that, there's a price. I forgave myself and went back to work in the General's office.

＝＝＝

When I was assigned to Fort Chaffee, the Army was contemplating an invasion of Cyprus or some arid country. We were scheduled for desert training, two months in the Mojave Desert: Operation Desert Strike. To initiate us, we were herded to the movie theater and shown Walt Disney's "The Living Desert." It was two hours of rattlesnakes, scorpions, spiders and all kinds of critters attacking and eating one another. Six hundred of us left the movie knowing: I'm gonna die!

By then I'd bonded with my company commander, Captain L. Chuck Banks, now a retired Lieutenant Colonel in Atlanta, and still my dear friend these forty-plus years later. He summoned me to be Company Clerk and we camouflaged my assignment on the morning report (since cryptographers were to be used for nothing other than that job).

In the desert it was overwhelming heat in the day and freezing at night. The young officers often secured a jeep to R&R (party) in some nearby, small Arizona town. To do so meant they saw me first and I assigned a driver—me. We had no social refreshments in our battalion in the desert.

Returning one night with a Captain driving and a young Corporal trying not to pass out in the back seat, we arrived at our camp about midnight. All the generators were off; the camp was pitch black. Some Sergeant was reporting to the CO from a distant field position. He was sleeping in the middle of my big Company Headquarters tent (which I had to myself) and I tumbled over him. That hurt! Alcohol, however, is great anesthesia. Off to dreamland.

The next morning I couldn't move my left arm. Even if I wiggled my fingers my entire shoulder and back went into horrid spasms. Captain Banks decided I needed to see the medics, those skeptics who knew these enlisted gold-brickers wanted out of the desert. They had no patience with alleged injuries.

"Take off your blouse."

"I can't. I can't lift or move my arm."

"Take it off or we'll cut it off."

"Cut it off."

"Cut off the T-shirt, too?"

"Cut it off."

Looking at my shoulder: "Oh Lord!" Double dislocation.

Not only am I assigned to the field hospital, but it was the only unit in the entire desert that (for whatever reason) had a beer tent. Once injured, we all knew it meant automatic reassignment back home for light duty.

We awaited the doctor's examination in the morning, spent the day in the beer tent, staggered to bed that night, and repeated it the following day. (Budweiser stock climbed five points. At 15 cents a can, we were wealthy.)

===

One morning the doctor told me: "I have great news for you."

"Yes, sir. Back to Fort Chaffee, light duty."

"No, we are flying in a physiotherapist from Los Angeles. This is the first time we'll perform physiotherapy in a field operation."

"And...?"

"Why, son, I'll have you back to your unit within the week."

(Not me, pal. I'm going home.)

This procedure required 'freezing' the shoulder, numbing it to pain and manipulating the arm—"Now this is the hazardous move, tell me if it causes any pain"—and moving my arm across my chest. "No, no pain."

When he left that tent, I threw more punches into the air with that numb, painless left arm than Mike Tyson in a championship fight.

(Forty years later, I'm paying a price for that physical abuse and asininity, but I was young, dumb and wanted to go home.)

Within forty-eight hours the doctor is amazed: "I want the therapy stepped up to twice a day." Twice a day I mimicked Mike Tyson. Finally: "I want no responsibility for this man's shoulder. Fly him out of here." I'm going home! Me against medicine—I won!

Our prop-driven airplane was forced to land in Taos, New Mexico due to thunderstorms. We all were driven to the post hospital for the night.

As we stood in line they asked about each injury. Whether it was a broken finger, ear infection or blister, the patient was assigned "bed rest." We are not getting hurt in their hospital; we will lay in bed until it's time to leave and we aren't welcome.

Somewhat to the rear of the line I eased the sling off my arm and stuffed it in my back pocket. Then I eased the arm in my front pocket to support it. "What's wrong with you, soldier?" My reply: "Nothing, sir. I'm just an NCO accompanying the group."

"Welcome, corporal. Want a bed now or would you like to know where the NCO Club is located?"

"Oh, I think a little nightcap would be appropriate."

I think I returned to the hospital (or managed to find it) about midnight.

We landed in San Antonio for those severely injured and assigned to Brooke Army Hospital. My name was called. "Sir, I'm on orders for Fort Chaffee. This is a mistake." I was told to tell the bus driver.

Bus driver: "I just drive. You tell them at Admissions."

Admissions: "I just admit you. Tell the male nurse on the ward."

Male Nurse: "You'll have to speak to the doctor in the morning."

Doctor: "Mistake? I'll be the judge of that. Bed rest!"

Now I'm trapped. I am not supposed to be in this hospital!

Four days later I was subjected to my PRE-Admissions physical. "Let's see, you're with Headquarters Company, 53d Signal Battalion, then Operation Desert Strike, then the Field Hospital and now light duty at Fort Chaffee. You *are not* to be in this hospital!"

"No, sir."

"Sometimes you drafted, enlisted men really irritate me. How long did you intend to let his error continue?"

"I just did what I was told, sir."

"You get to the uniform room, find one and get out of this hospital. We'll have a plane ride waiting for you at the airport."

"Yes, sir."

To have endured all that I did required compensation. The *only* uniform that seemed to fit me had Sergeant stripes on it. Another corporal was happy to drive me to the shared civilian-military airport, which, incidentally, had a bar! I had a three-hour wait for this short plane ride to Arkansas.

Nursing my first martini, a customer asked, "What happened to your arm, son?"

"Oh, I'd rather not talk about it."

"Viet Nam?"

"It's nothing to talk about."

"Bartender, give this soldier anything he wants and put it on my bill."

When I staggered down the stairs at Fort Chaffee, the Executive Officer was howling. "We can't find you for six days, and you show up both promoted and bombed. How the hell do you maneuver these things?"

"Just takes creativity, Lieutenant."

I was given a jeep, driver and an Army .45 to escort prisoners to court martial hearings. That was my light duty—99% of them were scared kids, usually charged with AWOL. There was no way I was shooting anyone, especially a kid, and there was no way he was shooting me! I escorted them for a month with an unloaded pistol.

━ ━

We had, in HQ Company, 53d Signal Battalion, a young, self-impressed and righteous 2d Lieutenant who was addicted to inflicting 'Article 15' punishment on soldiers. Article 15 was company, non-judicial punishment, rather like a misdemeanor. It seemed that once a week we summoned a soldier on the Lieutenant's complaint to ask if he'd accept Article 15 punishment, or if he insisted upon a court martial. Some choice!

No counseling by Captain Banks seem to lessen the Lieutenant's enthusiasm, and he always had some valid charge as it was worded.

The good Captain always issued thirty days restriction as punishment in lieu of fines or demotion. He was not enjoying any of this, but the Lieutenant would have been at Battalion HQ in a flash to complain about non-support of officers. The CO there was a bigger prima donna than the Lieutenant.

Thirty years later, at dinner, Chuck asked me, "Do you remember that Lieutenant and how many Article 15s that he forced upon me?"

"Sure I do. It was one."

"*One?!* It must have been twenty."

"No, Chuck, here's the way it worked. All of us assembled and the soldier accepted Article 15 punishment. He signed his copy, our copy, the battalion copy, the Adjutant General's copy and the personnel copy. You gave him his copy and I filed ours. Then I threw away all the others. At the end of thirty days, I threw away our copy. It took that first one for me to figure out the system."

"David, do you have any idea what the penalty for that would have been?"

"For what, Chuck? There was no paper trail. It faded in everyone's memory."

Someone had to administer justice, and a vision said it was me.

═ ━ ═

You never fool your mother. With a military childhood it didn't take much effort to win Outstanding Trainee in basic, and Soldier of the Month at two bases, answering all the questions before the review board. In fact, I won Soldier of the Quarter at Fort Chaffee.

The night before the award, five of us closed the NCO club in some vigorous partying. When Captain Banks escorted me to the General's office, he remarked, "I've never even met the General and I'm taking you? You look like hell!"

I got the award (a pen set) and my picture with the General was on the front page of the post paper. "My parents will, undoubtedly, be proud." My mother returned the paper, having circled my dark, sunken eyes and she illustrated it with a big question mark. She didn't understand that a young man drafted for two years joined his pals in as many parties as we could find and afford. Whether she did or not, she didn't approve.

Now that I'm working regularly with the Army, these are all good (or at least funny) memories of being young and irresponsible.

Just when you thought it was safe in the water:

A TRIBUTE TO MISSOURI MILITARY ACADEMY

In the TWA Training Center, the Manager of Ground Training was the late Glenn Hersh. There was a deeply affectionate bond between us. We were best friends, mutual confidants and Glenn deflected attention to my flaws more than I suppose I knew. When Glenn died, my heart was shattered.

We had a crisis, a bad mistake. Glenn and I were summoned to the Vice President's office and the reprimand was intense. I mastered fifteen new routines in that rug dance. Glenn sat quietly. He'd come to defend me if he could, but did not interrupt my handling of the issue.

Later, Glenn called me to his office: "There were seven people involved in that. Why didn't you reveal the whole truth, the others' involvement? You took the brunt of his wrath. Why?"

My reply: "You envision the worst possible outcome and are prepared to accept it without whining. How was it going to help me, and how would it have injured others, for me to involve them? They had me on the carpet. They were satisfied with one sacrifice. I gave it to them. At the Academy we called it loyalty to one another."

I rather imagined Colonel Charlie Stribling ('44), MMA President, smiling if he could have heard that exchange. He would not, however, have been surprised that I was still explaining "demerits." I may have been in the journalism, scholastic and speaking honor societies, but I was better known for absorbing the penalties of my antics.

MMA gave us standards, the rules for life and performance. Without rules, one never knew how far conduct deviated from them, or what standard summoned your return. (As I've said: If you didn't thoroughly know the rules, you couldn't break them with skill and hopefully, immunity.)

I attribute most of the genuine values on my life to MMA, where I arrived at age twelve. Later I had the honor to serve as Alumni President and as a member of the Board of Visitors.

The B-17 according to Burt Rutan:

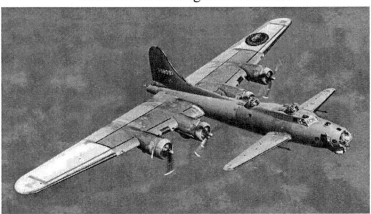

Confessional—"I Have Sinned"
As published in *Plane & Pilot* Magazine (2001)

Many thanks for the dozens of enjoyable emails which I get each month from our splendid *Plane & Pilot* partners. I've even gotten to share your fears and tears, especially over some of the dumb kind of things that just leap up and humiliate student pilots. ("Ohhh...the BLUE lights are the taxiway when you're landing!")

Some have had the audacity to ask me, an authentic airline pilot, what kind of mistakes I made as a student pilot. The Lord created the airline captain since He Himself could not be everywhere. Wouldn't you presuppose a flawless personal aviation history? Don't you know it takes only one airline pilot to change a light bulb? That's just to hold it, since the world revolves around him.

Well, I did (gasp!) make mistakes. I had a great flight instructor in Eddie Holloway, who had 10,000 hours some three decades ago. It's probably in a mega-count by now. He returned to flight training after retiring from the training department of a major corporation. All this was over thirty years ago! Wow, he was in his twenties; I was just a child, of course. With some statute of limitations certainly applicable, Eddie, I'll give you the story.

Back in the 1960s, we didn't have the rigid training curriculum we have now. Each CFI developed his own theme (or scheme) in the educational adventure. One of Eddie's back-burner concepts was VOR. "Anyone can fly a needle. You need basic skills, map reading, ground orientation, timing events. If you have electrical failure, that VOR is no help whatever."

Our first dual cross-country flight was, therefore, pilotage (map reading, checkpoints and time). This charitable chap then decided I needed a short, solo and confidence-building flight: Kansas City to Topeka and return. That's about 55 miles, perhaps. "I want you to land, have a cup of coffee, enjoy yourself and return."

All pilotage!

The weather was CAVU (Ceiling and Visibility Unlimited) and obviously so. But, I had to lay out the trip, point out a couple of checkpoints, discuss airport entry and all those trite tasks for this tiny adventure of no challenge. Eddie added, "That big river runs right from K.C. to Topeka. That's your safety element. I don't want you to just parallel that, but remember, find the river, turn east and you'll find home."

Eddie told me to enjoy myself. I took off, found the river, threw the maps behind me and used my inherent instincts of professional aviator: One river, one big city coming up and that's Topeka. Great sightseeing! No more complicated than parallel parking.

What we didn't know was that a fog bank lay over that river about 20 miles out of Kansas City. It was big and it was thick. I'm north of it; Topeka is south. "Can't reach the map. Wonder when I took off? Shucks, you can't miss a BIG city."

I flew…a long time. No Topeka. I flew longer….everything in fog south of me. Finally I found a city—and just about as big as Topeka ought to be. But I didn't remember any small mountain, which when I circled it, had big stones spelling out "Manhattan." That's about a hundred-plus miles from Kansas City, home of Kansas State University and its Wild Cats. This is called a 'small navigational error.' It is not to be compared to Lindbergh missing Paris by one-half mile.

Obviously it's time to head east. The sun was up, the fog dissipating and I even waved at Topeka as I passed it some time later. On that Hobbs meter, however, and the now sweat-stained watch on Eddie's wrist, far too much time has elapsed for this "short, confidence-building flight." Also, he needed the airplane.

It had to be a hot day. As I taxied to the ramp, I could see the heat waves rising around Eddie. "Where have you been?! WHERE have you been?!?" Here's the guy who insisted upon a prayer session before our flights, in which we prayed only for the safe return of Eddie. I have now returned an airplane undamaged and unbent, which he himself knew was an accomplishment.

"Ed, you told me to enjoy myself. I practiced lots of touch-and-goes in Topeka. Did great on my short field landings. Had coffee and came home. It was great. No, I did forget that. I didn't get my logbook signed." Get this: He's angry!

Now this skinny, young CFI (who is still disgustingly trim) throughout the entire course, considered me as penitence for more sins than he had lifetime breathing moments, *is angry*. Do you think I felt uplifted when your Pastor was with you for every dual flight I scheduled? Did you think I was so vague as to miss the 'goodbye' handshakes with the other CFIs? Hey, pal, you sat right beside me *crying*. I'm not oblivious. My Dad handled his genetic, endless crisis better than you. And it cost him more. I didn't turn me loose, you did! It sure wasn't a decision I would have made or taken responsibility for doing.

So, for all of you who had the unbelievable arrogance to believe I committed errors, that's one of the stories. For Eddie: GOTCHA!! Didn't know that for thirty years, did you, pallie?

—==—

What a joy aviation has been. A little boy told me, "When I grow up, I want to be an airline pilot." I had to tell him frankly, "Son, you just can't do both." From licensing in land and sea planes, helicopters, gyroplanes, gliders and jets, Eddie Holloway laid the foundation for abundant happiness and blessings in my life. I just wasn't one of his at the time.

As my airline career closed, I remember one specific day sliding into the left seat of a passenger jet. Never thought I'd be here. Never hoped for it to end. My mind inventoried the fun and flaws of an aviation vocational life, from its beginning to its imminent closure. I remember thinking, "Thanks, Eddie." Then I called for the Before Starting Engines Checklist.

Eddie taught me to land, always emphasizing: "One airplane at a time!"

The worst case: One can't see *down*, the other can't see *up*. Still—unforgivable.

MY RETIREMENT FLIGHT AND EMERGENCY

There are two successful ways to end an airline career: You never had an emergency and never met the Chief Pilot.

My retirement flight was uneventful into the second day of a five-day trip. We were delayed in Atlanta for four hours for some reason I do not recall. This meant a midnight arrival back in St. Louis and arriving in Wichita somewhere near 3 a.m.

A heavy thunderstorm line was between STL and ICT. Our routing was St. Louis, up into mid-Iowa, and down to Wichita. Having taught the use of airborne weather radar for many years, I was manipulating the radar to find a better way. My superb co-captain (copilot) Tom Hernon was flying the plane. After a couple of radar checks for validity, I said, "I've got it, Tom. There's a way through that line. I'll give you the headings. Turbulence penetration speed, anti-ice on, ignition on, and turn left 30 degrees."

Once committed, it was rough, tough and rainy. Lightning flashes were plentiful left and right. My head was down, still using radar and giving minor vectors to Tom. A red light illuminated just above me. "What the hell is that?" The overhead annunciator panel light indicated "Cabin Pressure Loss." The cabin was climbing about 700

FPM, already through 10,000 feet. At 14,000 feet, all the passenger oxygen masks would drop. That was inevitable now.

We donned the oxygen masks, ran a couple of checks and I said, "Take it down. I'll talk to ATC and the passengers."

"Center, I need an immediate clearance to 10,000 feet."

"Roger, TWA, cleared to 10,000. Do you have an emergency?" (Imagine the paperwork in answering that question. What's HE going to do to help me?)

"No emergency. Leaving Flight Level 280 for 10."

Crash, bang, lightning, heavy rain, 5000 FPM descent rate. "Ladies and gentlemen, this is the captain. Please follow the instructions of our cabin team. We have lost pressure and are descending to a safe environment. If there were something to fear, you'd hear it in my voice, and you don't. Just trust us to keep you safe, and we'll not disappoint you."

"TWA, state your fuel on board, souls on board and intentions."

"Stand by, Center—now I want 8000." I'd recalled the elderly on board and some young children, thinking the lower altitude was preferable.

"Roger, TWA cleared to 8000. State your intentions, fuel on board and souls on board."

"I TOLD YOU to stand by. I'll talk to you in due time."

We arrived at 8000 feet, completed whatever checklist cleanup was required, calmed the passengers further and we were flying 250 knots in moderate rain. I picked up the microphone and said, "Okay, Center, TWA and I'm ready to get a clearance to Kansas City." Silence. We are now too low to communicate on that frequency.

"Tom, take up a heading of 240 degrees. I think that's about Kansas City." I spun the radio dial from frequency to frequency: "Anyone hear TWA?" Finally a United flight heard us, relayed our position to Center and got us a low altitude frequency. We were cleared to MCI.

On approach something was banging in the plane, something loose, and it sounded like it was on top the cockpit. (relay of sound, actually). Since Tom had the feel for the airplane, it was best to let him fly and for me to attempt to analyze the problem. With gear extension and flap settings, he was to tell me any ill effect, and I'd return to the previous position. (It turned out to be a blown duct in the rear of the airplane; the banging was being transmitted by the fuselage.)

The arrival was uneventful. We got a new airplane, even relief pilots, and arrived in Wichita about 0400.

The next morning the message light was blinking on my telephone. I dialed to receive it. It was the Chief Pilot. "They woke me at 4 a.m. to tell me about your emergency. I asked who was the captain. I decided if you needed excitement on your retirement trip, that was your option. I went back to bed. Good luck."

Fortunately by not declaring an emergency (nor could they have helped me with this one), I was not delayed by a pile of paperwork and reports. At least the next and final day went without incident as reported by my dear friend Rod Machado who shared the cockpit with us.

RETIREMENT FLIGHT

Originally appeared on AOPA's Web site (www.aopa.org)

By Rod Machado

I thought the readers of these web articles might enjoy reading about an experience I had last month (November 1998).

Captain Dave Gwinn is a columnist for *Plane & Pilot* magazine and the radar authority I've used as a resource for several of these AOPA web articles. Dave is a dear friend who has an awesome sense of humor. We're always kidding each other. An opportunity to fly in the cockpit on an airline captain's last flight is rare, and it is especially rare when the captain is a dear friend. I was fortunate enough to have that experience with Captain Dave Gwinn.

On November 12th, I showed up at the TWA gate in St. Louis as Captain Dave was punching in the door combination to board his DC-9.

From 20 feet I yelled, "Hey, let's see your boarding pass, mister."

I must have startled Dave because he patted his left shirt pocket, in search of either a boarding pass, chewing gum or heart palpitations.

He had no idea I was going to be there, much less ride in the cockpit. We hugged like lost buddies. Then I showed him my cockpit authorization. Of course, I showed it to him from a distance, then pretended to read from it.

"Dave," I quipped, "it says here that I'm not only allowed to ride in the cockpit on both flights, but that I can fly the airplane if I really want to."

Suddenly Dave began patting his left shirt pocket again.

"Hey, I was just kidding about that boarding pass," I said.

"I'm not looking for a boarding pass," responded Dave. "I'm checking for heart palpitations."

And that's the way the flight began.

For years I've been telling everyone that Dave calls me from the cockpit just so I can talk him down. Well, let me quash the latest rumor. I didn't go along on his last flight just to save long distance telephone charges. I went along to share the experience with a good friend. (Special thanks to my friend and fellow author TWA Capt. Wally Roberts (Ret.), for his helping arrange my flight.)

We departed St. Louis to Chicago on a round trip flight Thursday morning, November 12th. On board were several of Dave's friends: Anne Umphrey, Shelley Rose (a TWA F/O), John Miller (his best buddy) and Henrietta, John's wife. Dave's copilot, Tom Hernon, had specifically bid to fly with Dave on this flight. Several other TWA admirers also bid for this copilot slot but Tom beat them to it and wasn't about to give it up.

As we taxied for takeoff, Dave, true to form, commenced giving me the business. "Hmmm, what does that switch do?" he mused out loud. Nice try, Dave. Then I informed him that I probably wouldn't see much of his takeoff since it's difficult to see things with my hands over my eyes. Well, it was obvious that I wasn't about to nonplus the master with my shenanigans.

The takeoff was spectacular. The mechanical action of lifting tens of thousands of pounds of metal into the air with a simple curl of the yoke is an impressive sight. Dave rolled the airplane into a 30 degree left bank, flipped a few switches and we were on our way to Chicago. As my friend guided his airplane through a departure, I was filled with an enormous sense of pride. "I know this man to be a gifted teacher, skillful communicator and masterful writer," I thought. "Now I've finally witnessed him do what he's done most of his life, and do it so well: fly airplanes."

It's in the nature of an instrument instructor to watch the needles. I did. And they weren't moving. Not that I'm surprised by an airline pilot's ability to hold altitude, heading and airspeed, but there was such an economy of motion in Dave's actions. Every movement seemed purposeful and calculated, not wasted.

Dave made it look easy.

So easy, in fact, that I said to myself, "Hey, I can fly this thing just like Dave," but I know better. Experience taught me a long time ago that a master makes a complex task look effortless. The illusion of effortless action is the ultimate manifestation of skill. When I leaned over and said, "Captain, you make this look so easy," I realized that I had just given Dave the highest compliment one pilot can give another.

Dave was the essence of professionalism. I even mentioned this to him and commented on how surprised I was that his use of the phrase "Center, who-dah-man?" would be so well received by ATC on every call. (OK, that really didn't happen, but all the other stuff did. Honest!)

Out of 12,000 feet, we approached a vertical wall of clouds. Dave quipped, "These are the times that make me wish I had an instrument rating." He was at it again. In response, I desperately wanted to say, "Ah, captain, I think the PA system was active when you said that." But I didn't. I couldn't stop laughing long enough.

Enroute, Copilot Tom Hernon informed Dave that he could expect a right crosswind at Chicago. Dave slapped his left leg, patted his right hand, then joked, "OK, that means we gotta push this leg and twist that arm."

Hey, I did my homework. I was prepared for my pal's mischievousness. You see, I've heard the stories about Captain Dave pointing out the Euphrates and Nile rivers to unsuspecting passengers on the St. Louis to Chicago route. I wasn't about to fall for that ruse. Besides, I was too busy looking for the pyramids. On the return flight Dave announced the presence of the large Gateway Arch in St. Louis, which he announced "commemorates Missouri's annual croquet tournament."

The return trip was too quick. "I could get to like it up here," I thought, "This is fun." Yes, it is fun, especially when Dave's the captain. ATC gave us permission to level off at cloud-top level where we skipped along puffs of stratus. "Isn't this beautiful?" Dave asked. "Isn't it simply beautiful?" A pilot who can still say that after decades of flying is someone who has never lost sight of what flying is all about.

Pulling the DC-9 into a steep climb, Dave pointed skyward toward the wispy contrails of an invisible airplane. "Look up there," Dave said. "That's the Hale-Bopp comet. Can you see it, Rod?"

"Oh, I'm sorry, Dave," I replied. "I was busy looking outside trying to find the Euphrates River. And I'm really upset that I didn't get to see the Sphinx either." And that's the way it went on the trip home.

There were quiet moments, too. These were moments of existential reverie which stayed cockpit banter, moments when I mulled over the thought that Dave would never fly as a TWA pilot again. "This was the last time," I thought, "the last time he'll land this airplane, the last time he'll move those throttles, the last time he'll pull into this gate." It was sad in that way, but then I remembered that the general aviation community now gets Dave full time. TWA's loss is our gain!

As we approached the terminal, I peeked out the window at the jetway. Lining the walls were Dave's friends a gathering of fellow pilots, admirers and well-wishers. Among them were several young pilots who credit Dave for helping them with their airline careers. "How sad, how sad, how sad," I thought. "All those people out there and not one of them is wearing a Groucho Marx nose and glasses. How could I ever forgive myself for letting that happen?"

Many years ago a young boy said to Dave, "When I grow up I want to be an airline pilot." To which Dave replied, "I'm sorry, but you can't do both."

It's obvious that Dave is like many of us. He's a pilot who has never lost his passion for aviation and never lost sight of what flying is all about.

This was one of the very best times I've had in aviation. I was proud to share it with my friend and the friends of my friend. It's an experience I'll never forget.

Saying Goodbye to the Job

As published in *Plane & Pilot* Magazine (2000)

About two issues ago I discussed "Is Aviation in Your Future?" I have been inundated with email since then. It is always a compliment to hear from our subscribers, writing for advice you thought I had.

Another aspect of an aviation career, often a volatile topic, is the mandatory retirement as a pilot of Part 121 airliners at age 60. In 1958, the FAA Czar dictated the regulation, imposed it. The FAA declared that age 60 neutralized anyone's ability to cope with complicated, heavy, fast technology. New airplanes-old men-impending disaster. Vocational euthanasia.

Prior to most fleets being saturated with two-pilot cockpits, an age 60 pilot could revert to flight engineer for some length of time. That never interested me. At age 60, however, that pilot could not be a Captain or First Officer.

Over the years there have been lawsuits and lobbying to eliminate this antiquated regulation, all for naught. It would seem to me that legislators have one mindset: "Age 60 is too young, but it's still safe. If I sponsor something beyond that and there's an accident, it might be an over-60 incapacitated pilot. Therefore, it is politically safe to let it stand as it is. Not my problem."

The pilots' union's position was particularly amusing to me. They are opposed to extending a pilot's career beyond age 60. A pilot's entire career is governed by a seniority number. When a pilot retires and friends meet the last flight, the young ones really have to resist cheering the vacant seniority number. Sometimes one seniority number can be the difference between a layoff or upgrading to Captain today or six months later.

The pilots' unions are made up of about 60-to-maybe-75% "young" pilots who want those gray eagles gone! That retiring birdman is not going to be paying any more dues; the junior pilots will be paying them for years to come. That retiring gent will also be replaced by a new hire who will also pay dues for a few decades. Guess who is dispensable? It seems to me that money dictated, not the practicality of an age 60 pilot being healthy and competent. Alas, all those dues, all those years! "Dave, we no longer know ya." However, you have to admit it's 'democratic.'

I didn't retire with joy or bitterness. To anticipate such change was intimidating. I hung up my Captain's uniform for the last time with moist eyes: It's all over. I was no longer due anywhere, no schedule. No one needed my talents or me. The feeling was rejection. We had seen contemporaries shuffle off to an early grave because 'being a Captain' was their identity in life, their self-worth.

I was fortunate. I had the magazines, public speaking dates, trying to write three long-on-the-back-burner books simultaneously, and traveling worldwide to teach radar seminars as a consultant to Honeywell Systems Training. I was a golf addict. (If I can eliminate only 32 strokes from my game, I'll probably turn pro.) I also absorbed the philosophy that my daughter grew tired of hearing: Your job is what you do—it is not who you are. It only pays money, which enables you to do what you want; it is not your value or identity in this world.

A soothing perspective altered my disposition long ago. The Age 60 rule, when introduced, was social change (of status, entitlement and privilege). We've never had social change without penalty. Who suffered with the elimination of serfdom in Europe and the godless slavery in our country? The land barons and plantation owners. They may not have been the same individuals who profited those many decades, but they represented the *same class of society which benefited.*

Had there not been an Age 60 rule when I was a teenager in military school, I might not have been hired some years later. Hundreds of sad and protesting age 60 pilots departed as kids like me arrived to take their place. I benefited. So my Age 60 date was my time to graciously repay the gain, surrender the job to a younger pilot, as I had been thirty years earlier. As opposed to an after-the-fact and penalized social class, I had both gained and forfeited under the same system. That's equitable.

Like all pilots over the years, I watched the projections and bids get published, anticipating when my number sufficed to fly captain. I read the retirement notices with satisfaction: Five more gone! It was like the old joke, asking a first officer, "What would you do, mid-Atlantic, if you learned the captain had expired in flight?" The answer: "I'd try to get him out of MY seat." Not many of my contemporaries were opposing or seeking legal action about the Age 60 rule until they themselves were age 55 or older.

Summed up: Is the present Age 60 rule reasonably founded and fair? No, it's ridiculous. We forfeit decades of experience in every airline, discarding pilots in superb health. We always had one or more qualified pilots in cockpits. Nothing was doomed by the incapacitation of the captain.

To be frank, if the Age 60 rule had been revoked the day before I retired, I would not have been the poster boy; my new entitlement a source of rage among young pilots who expected a seniority number vacated. I would not have ended a wonderful career with resentment and bitterness around me from my younger peers.

You can imagine my philosophy is not popular among some of my retired friends. I retired with sadness; my time had passed, but not with resentment. In 1969 I benefited and balanced the equation in 1999. I'd gotten to do it all, not only with the airlines, but flew and/or instructed in airplanes, seaplanes, gliders, helicopters and gyroplanes. I'd been writing for fine magazines, speaking at rewarding conventions, teaching all over the world, and even instructing within TWA's pilot training center for a decade. I'd been blessed. I'd wish every captain to retire with the warmth of memories and airline friends, the blessing of activity awaiting them, and the happiness that I've enjoyed before and after hanging up that uniform. (I still put on the gilded hat once in a while...thought about sleeping in it...just to remember.)

DESTINATION
By Capt. Mike Larkin, TWA (Retired)

I hope there's a place way up in the sky,
Where airmen can go when they die.
A place where a guy can buy a cold beer,
For a friend and a comrade, whose memory is dear.
A place where no doctor or lawyer can tread,
Nor a management type would ere be caught dead.
Just a quaint little place, kind of dark, full of smoke,
Where they like to sing loud and love a good joke.
The kind of place where a lady could go,
And feel safe and protected by the men she would know.
There must be a place where old airmen go,
When the paining is finished, and their airspeed gets low.
Where the whiskey is old, and the women are young,
And songs about flying and dying are sung.
Where you'd see all the fellows who'd flown West before,
And they'd call out your name, as you came through the
    door.
Who would buy you a drink, if your thirst should be bad,
And relate to the others, "He was quite a good lad."
And then through the mist, you'd spot an old guy,
You had not seen in years, though he taught you to fly.
He'd nod his old head, and grin ear to ear,

And say "Welcome, my son, I'm pleased that you're here."
For this is a place where true fliers come,
When their journey is over, and the war has been won.
They've come here at last to be safe and alone,
From the government clerk, and the management clone,
Politicians and lawyers, the Feds and the noise,
Where all hours are happy, and these good ole boys,
Can relax with a cool one, and well deserved rest,
This is Heaven, my son...You've passed your last test.

EPILOGUE

Having discovered *Airways and Airwaves ~ Stories I Tell To Friends*, an anecdotal book including humorous vignettes of his innumerable experiences involving aviation, it seemed only fitting that someone share the facts of who is this character Dave Gwinn. That said, Dave granted permission to write a brief comment as an epilogue to this wonderful compilation of true short stories. Knowing Dave through decades gives one an edge in understanding this extraordinary man's genesis, genius and continually growing persona.

First, in all my years of personal and professional association, Dave may be the most honorable man I know. Always the truth, the whole truth and nothing but the truth no matter how it hurts him. Dave's pictures would be plastered throughout any good dictionary next to words like honesty, integrity, humor, courage and intelligence. Speaking of the last, on a whim, Dave took the Mensa Test in 1972, not only easily qualifying in the top 2% IQ level, but also in the 1% IQ level required by the Intertel organization. Perhaps that's why an active mind sometimes contributed chaos when the rigidity of policy required comic relief.

Although verification is easily made for all of Gwinn's exceptional qualities, none is more impressive than his

Heart of Gold. Dave is a genuine treasure not only to me and those who know him personally, but to the tens of thousands who have benefited from the world's foremost weather radar expert. He has surely saved thousands of lives through his weather radar education and entertained even more with his special brand of humor.

This book highlights the wisdom and wit of aviation experience as seen through the eyes of one of aviation's finest, and I am proud to know this great man.

Steve Lanard
TWA Captain (Retired)
Captain Instructor/CheckAirman: 727, 757/767, L10
Captain: Lear Jet
Aircraft Dispatcher
FAA Control Tower Operator
USAF Air Traffic Control Certificate

I hope you've enjoyed these memories, and you'll share some of yours with me. I'm a bit older now, but...

...let's not forget: Once a Captain, always a Captain:

It's my book and I'm not closing it without sharing my precious daughter with you, Seana Marie and her husband, Taz: